FAITH, DOUBT, AND COURAGE

in Fifteen Great People
of Faith and What
We Can Learn
From Them

FAITH, DOUBT, AND COURAGE

in Fifteen Great People
of Faith and What
We Can Learn
From Them

JOHN R. TYSON

WIPF & STOCK · Eugene, Oregon

Wipf and Stock Publishers
199 W 8th Ave, Suite 3
Eugene, OR 97401

Faith, Doubt, and Courage in 15 Great People of Faith
and What We Can Learn From Them
By Tyson, John R.
Copyright©2008 by Tyson, John R.
ISBN 13: 978-1-62564-266-0
Publication date 8/31/2013
Previously published by Abingdon, 2008

Contents

Introduction

Welcome to *Faith, Doubt, and Courage in Fifteen Great People of Faith and What We Can Learn From Them*! In these pages you will meet fifteen of my favorite Christian friends from the past as you read about their faith journeys. These women and men have been a significant source of encouragement to me over the years as I have tried to live the life of Christian faith and discipleship. They have been faithful partners in dialogue and spiritual direction whose Christian witness has often challenged, refined, and corrected my own.

Each of these people is a "saint" in the sense that they were "in Christ" and were in the process of becoming a "new creation." In their lives (as in our own lives) we catch a glimpse of the old passing away and the new life in Christ becoming a reality (2 Corinthians 5:17). But none of these people was so much a "saint" that they were impervious to doubt, failure, and criticism. Indeed, like us, each of these people had profound strengths and debilitating weaknesses. It is precisely their struggle to be faithful witnesses for Jesus Christ in the face of genuine challenges and deficiencies that is probably most instructive for us.

In some cases our own faith crises may strongly parallel those faced by Augustine, Dame Julian, Martin Luther, or Mother Teresa. In other instances the challenges we face pale in comparison to those of Perpetua; Dietrich Bonhoeffer; or Martin Luther King, Jr. Often their courage leaves us breathless and at the same time fortified in our own faith. Observing the

7

profound faith of these people in the context of these soul-straining situations helps us mark out our own path of faithfulness.

So often we feel as though we are the only Christian person who has been challenged by doubts, by a deep sense of spiritual coldness, by a restless heart that yearns for something other than God; or perhaps we are weighed down by a sense of duty that robs our Christianity of joy and spontaneity so that "life in the Spirit" seems like a faint memory or a distant hope. We feel alone, surrounded by defeat and by our own inadequacies. In some measure, I think, it helps us to know that Mother Teresa, Augustine, and Martin Luther—great spiritual heroes of the Christian faith—experienced similar trials and were victorious over them. Like Athanasius, Catherine of Siena, Francis and Clare of Assisi, or the Wesley brothers, we have wished we could make a difference in the direction of the Church. Like John Calvin or Karl Barth, we sometimes are desperate to know what God wills for us or to hear afresh from God in a profoundly personal way. Like Anselm and Aquinas, our hearts and minds sometimes seem out of sync; and we long for a faith that seems more credible and intellectually sound.

What follows is my own compilation of what the writer of the Letter to the Hebrews termed a "great cloud of witnesses" (Hebrews 12:1). I hope that, like the remarkable catalog of heroes and heroines that writer drew from the Hebrew Scriptures, the story of these heroic Christian witnesses enables "us also [to] lay aside every weight and the sin that clings so closely, and...run with perseverance the race that is set before us, looking to Jesus the pioneer and perfecter of our faith" (Hebrews 12:1-2).

John. R. Tyson

I

Vibia Perpetua
(ca. 181–203)

Faith and Courage

We sometimes feel that we are forced to make hard decisions because of our Christian faith. "Should I attend that movie?" "Can I continue my friendship with this person even though he or she involves me in feelings or actions that are inconsistent with my faith?" These sorts of situations, however, pale in comparison to the challenges the early Christians faced. In the reading that follows, an early Christian named Perpetua finds herself in the midst of a tragic dilemma. Her story, because it is so tragic, is quite challenging to the modern reader. But it also offers us a powerful example of how faith can triumph over doubt and express itself in courage.

* * * *

The hot, North African sun beat down on Vibia Perpetua as she stood before the Roman proconsul Hilarion. She and five Christian companions were on trial for their lives. Barely twenty-two years old, this young wife and new mother faced a terrible dilemma. She had to decide whether she should continue to profess her faith in Jesus Christ and suffer a horrible death or deny Christ so that she could go home to her husband and family and live to rear her infant son. What events could bring a person to a situation in which she or he would have to make such a terrible decision?

Ever since the reign of Emperor Trajan, around AD 112, simply being a Christian was a capital crime. People who were charged with being a Christian were dragged before a Roman official and asked to affirm, "Caesar is Lord." In the polytheistic Roman world, it was a small matter to offer worship to Caesar by lighting a stick of incense at the altar of Jupiter. The Roman gods and goddesses did not require exclusive loyalty from their devotees, and adding the Emperor to the long list of deities a person served was seen as a simple act of pledging one's allegiance to the Roman state.

Christians, however, saw this matter quite differently than their pagan contemporaries. Since Jesus Christ had exclusive claim on their lives, they refused to share the glory that belonged only to him with any other figure. On this basis, then, the Roman state began publicly executing Christians for treason. Enough Christians were willing to deny Christ in order to spare their own lives that this wave of persecution caused a leadership crisis in the early church. Should a person who renounced Christ be accepted back into the Christian fellowship? Should a pastor who denied Christ be allowed to lead a local congregation or administer the Christian sacraments? Many Christians chose death over compromise, however. Their martyrdom also contributed to the leadership crisis in the early church by robbing it of the service of the most faithful and courageous Christians.

Christians, as the Romans saw them, were people who deserved death. They were regarded as being socially deviant, narrow-minded, and unpatriotic people. When given an opportunity to affirm their loyalty to the Roman state and Emperor, they refused, saying they could worship only the one God. They did not join their fellow Romans in the public festivals dedicated to the Olympian gods. They did not participate in the lewd rites associated with the pagan mystery religions. In fact, no one saw the Christians worship anyone or anything. Their avoidance of the popular holidays and their antipathy toward idols made them seem like atheists to their pagan contemporaries. Thousands of people shouted, "Away with the atheists!" as Christians met with horrible deaths in Roman coliseums.

Terrible rumors were circulating about the private practices of the Christians. Most people believed that they were complete hypocrites who claimed to live morally pure lives yet greeted each other with a "holy kiss" (See Romans 16:16.). While no one had ever seen anything amiss at their "love feasts" (1 Corinthians 11:17-34), people imagined that Christians secretly participated in lurid orgies. There were even rumors that the

Christians were cannibals who stole babies and baked their bodies into the ceremonial bread Christians served during their clandestine rites. "Eat the body," they were heard to whisper to one another.

Such people were seen as undermining the very fabric of Roman society. Emperors persecuted them, with greater and lesser degrees of vigor, as a way of protecting their own authority on the one hand and uniting the people against a common foe on the other. Hence, the Christians often became governmental scapegoats for failed policies and failed crops, defeat in battle, and natural disasters because they had turned people's attention away from the traditional gods and goddesses that had supposedly made Rome so strong in the pre-Christian era.

Vibia Perpetua faced her horrible choice because the current Roman emperor, Septimus Severus (145–211), had begun to enforce the old laws against Christianity with renewed vigor. Since Carthage, in North Africa (Perpetua lived in or near Carthage.), was a hot bed of Christian religious devotion, it became a focal point for persecution. The Emperor was convinced that Christianity was an unpatriotic and barbaric religion, and he intended to stamp it out. Perpetua had recently professed Christian faith and was in the process of joining the church when she was arrested in 202. The fact that she was arrested along with four other members of her church membership class ("catechumens") suggests that someone may have followed one of them to or from one of their clandestine instructional meetings and reported the group to the Roman officials.

Perpetua was a literate and cultured young woman, who kept a diary of her days in prison. In it we have a detailed record of her sufferings and her courageous faith.

Soon after her arrest, Perpetua's father, who was not a Christian, came to her and begged her to renounce her new faith so that she might avoid the death sentence that surely awaited her.

"Father," she said to him, "do you see here, for example, this vase, or pitcher, or whatever it is?"

"I see it," he replied.

"Can it be named anything else than what it really is?" she asked.

"No," he said.

"So I also cannot be called anything else than what I am, a Christian," she replied.[1]

Perpetua's words threw her father into a rage, so fierce (she said), that he "came at me as though to tear out my eyes."[2]

What inner resources did Perpetua draw on as she resolved not to deny Christ? We can only imagine, but it seems likely that Jesus' words were a source of direction and comfort to her. Commitment to Christ was rightly seen as a call to self-denial, personal discipleship, and cross bearing. As Jesus said, "If any want to become my followers, let them deny themselves and take up their cross and follow me. For those who want to save their life will lose it, and those who lose their life for my sake will find it. For what will it profit them if they gain the whole world but forfeit their life? Or what will they give in return for their life?" (Matthew 16:24-25). Jesus' promise, from Matthew 10:32-33, may have resonated in her heart and mind: "Everyone therefore who acknowledges me before others, I will also acknowledge before my Father in heaven; but whoever denies me before others, I also will deny before my Father in heaven."

The courageous affirmation of Jesus' first disciples found its echo in her actions: "Peter said to him [Jesus], 'Even though I must die with you, I will not deny you.' And so said all the disciples" (Matthew 26:35). The apostle Paul's triumphant words may have also encouraged her: "For to me, living is Christ and dying is gain" (Philippians 1:21). All Christians who believed in the Resurrection and in everlasting life could embrace the apostle's courageous and hopeful words: "When this perishable body puts on imperishability, and this moral body puts on immortality, then the saying that is written will be fulfilled:

"Death has been swallowed up in victory."
"Where, O death is your victory?
Where, O death, is your sting?"
(1 Corinthians 15:54-55)

For a few days, Perpetua's father stayed away; and during that time she was baptized. She recalled that she asked nothing from the waters of baptism "except endurance of physical suffering."[3]

During her initial imprisonment, Perpetua suffered severely. "I was terrified," she wrote, "because never before had I experienced such darkness. What a terrible day! Because of crowded conditions and rough treatment by the soldiers the heat was unbearable. My condition was aggravated by my anxiety for my baby."[4] But soon the deacons from her church visited her; and then her brother, who was also a Christian, visited. Perpetua's spirits gradually lifted, though she remained in agony about the plight of her infant son.

Soon her mother was permitted to visit Perpetua, and she brought the child with her. He was weak from hunger, and Perpetua was able to nurse him. As if it were an answer to her prayers, Perpetua was allowed to keep her son with her during the imprisonment; and he regained his strength and vitality through her care. Her brother suggested that Perpetua should ask God for a vision, indicating whether she would be condemned or freed as a result of her upcoming trial. She agreed with his suggestion and prayed to God for direction.

During her prayer Perpetua was given a vision of a long "bronze ladder of extraordinary height" that reached all the way to heaven; it was so narrow that only one person at a time could ascend it. There were weapons attached to the sides of the ladder. Crouching beneath the ladder was "a monstrous dragon who threatened those climbing up and tried to frighten them from [the] ascent." The first person to climb the ladder was Saturus, the deacon who taught her church membership class. He had surrendered himself to the Romans so that he could be with his students in prison; now—in her dream—he led them toward heaven. After he reached the top of the ladder, Saturus called on Perpetua to follow him. "Be careful not to be bitten by the dragon," he warned. Perpetua recalled, "I told him that in the name of Jesus Christ the dragon could not harm me. At this the dragon slowly lowered its head as though afraid of me. Using its head as the first step, I began my ascent." At the top of the ladder she found an "immense garden," where she was met by a "grey-haired man dressed like a shepherd." Surrounded by thousands of people dressed in white robes, he was tending the sheep and making cheese. When he saw Perpetua, he said, "Welcome, my child," and gave her a piece of cheese to eat. As she ate the sweet cheese, the white-robed multitude surrounded her, saying, "Amen." "I awoke," she wrote, "still tasting the sweet cheese. I immediately told my brother about the vision, and we both realized that we were to experience the sufferings of martyrdom. From then on we gave up any hope in this world."[5]

A few days later, rumors circulated through Carthage that the Christians would be brought to trial. Perpetua's father visited her once again, and again he sought to persuade her to worship Caesar and live. "Consider your brothers; consider your mother and your aunt; consider your son who cannot live without you," he urged her. "Give up your stubbornness before you destroy all of us. None of us will be able to speak freely if anything happens to you."[6]

She responded to her father's pleas and tears by trying to comfort him. "Whatever God wants at this tribunal will happen," she told him; "for remember that our power comes not from ourselves but from God."[7]

Her father was "utterly dejected" as he left her.[8]

One day, as the prisoners were eating a meager lunch, guards rushed in and hurried them off to a public hearing. When the word spread throughout Carthage that the Christians were coming to trial, the city forum was filled with a large crowd. As she was brought up the prisoner's platform, Perpetua saw her father elbow his way to the front of the crowd. He had her son in his arms as he grabbed hold of her and tried to drag her from the steps. "Have pity on your son!" he begged.[9]

At this point the Roman proconsul, Hilarion, also addressed Perpetua: "Have pity on your father's grey head; have pity on your infant son; offer sacrifice for the emperor's welfare."

But she answered simply, "I will not."

Hilarion then asked, "Are you a Christian?"

She answered, "I am a Christian."

Once again, her father tried to dissuade her from professing her faith; but now Hilarion ordered him to be removed and beaten with rods for interfering in the hearing.

"My father's injury hurt me as much as if I myself had been beaten," she recalled. "I grieved because of his pathetic old age."[10]

Then Hilarion passed sentence on Perpetua and the other prisoners charged with being Christians—all of whom refused to offer worship to the Emperor. They were condemned to death by wild beasts in the public arena.

After the prisoners had been returned to the jail to await their execution, Perpetua asked one of the church deacons who was not a prisoner to go to her father's house and bring her son to her so that she could nurse him. But her father refused to give up the child. When the deacon reported this to Perpetua, she found that her milk had dried up. She took this to be a sign from God that her son no longer needed her nursing and would be able to survive without her. During the next few days, Perpetua had several more visions that had the effect of confirming her faith in God and encouraging her steadfastness in the course of action she had chosen. The visions seemed to be designed to strengthen her and inform her about what was going to happen to her in the arena. They also had the effect of alleviating her anxiety about her child and family.

Several days later, on March 7, 203, the Christians were taken in chains to the arena to participate in the public "games." It was decided that Perpetua and the other female prisoner, Felicitas (who was her personal slave and friend), should be dispatched by an animal that matched their own gender: They would be attacked by a mad cow. Felicitas had given birth while in prison, only two days prior to her execution. So when the two young women were stripped, wrapped in nets, and led into the arena, the audience recoiled in horror at the sight of two young women modestly trying to cover themselves—the one having so recently given birth that her breasts were dripping with milk.

Guards were quickly sent to retrieve the women and to dress them in loosely fitting gowns. On returning to the arena, the women began to pray as the wild cow tossed Perpetua through the air and trampled on her and then on Felicitas. As they helped each other to their feet, Perpetua spoke words of encouragement: "Remain strong in your faith and love one another. Do not let our excruciating suffering become a stumbling block for you."[11] Leopards, bears, and other fierce animals had been released to kill the other catechumens who were also in the arena.

As the Christians stood together in prayer, the animals refused to attack them; so gladiators were dispatched to finish them off. True to Perpetua's vision, the first to enter heaven by way of the sword was Saturus; Perpetua soon followed him. As the former slave (Felicitas) and her former mistress (Perpetua) stood side by side as sisters in Christ, a guard struck Perpetua with his sword. But the weapon missed its mark. Striking her in the ribs, it failed to inflict a mortal wound. After screaming in pain, Perpetua calmly "took the gladiator's trembling hand [and] and guided it to her throat."[12]

Many of the guards and spectators who viewed the martyrs' courageous sufferings found that begrudged admiration had replaced the hatred they held in their hearts against the Christians. So it was, as the North African church father Tertullian (ca. 200) wrote, "The blood of the martyrs is the seed of the church."[13]

Perpetua's story was a source of tremendous encouragement to the early church during the next century of persecution and thereafter. Her example as a courageous disciple of Christ and a martyr caused her to be one of the first women to be accorded special acclaim as a "saint." March 7, the date of her death, was celebrated as a day of solemn remembrance and dedication. As superstition gradually mingled with Christian spirituality, young women and men sometimes wore religious medals that bore her image and the inscription, "Saint Perpetua, pray for us."

Perpetua's heroic act leaves us breathless. Perhaps we cannot echo an "Amen" to her willingness to profess Christ unto death at the cost of leaving behind her newborn child. But whether we agree with her decision or not, we can certainly savor the vitality of her faith and recognize in it the same powerful resource that can help us face hard decisions in our own lives. It is also worth noting that God confirmed Perpetua's decision by giving her extraordinary visions that calmed her heart and pointed her way forward. We too can rely on God to confirm our faith and guide us by the power of the Word and the Holy Spirit.

Prayer

Gracious God, thinking about the challenges Perpetua faced reminds me of the soul-straining situations Christians in various parts of the world encounter today. Be especially near to my brothers and sisters in Christ who are enduring persecution. Grant them the courage to keep the faith even in a hostile context. Grant me the faith to turn to you anew for help and courage in the dilemmas I face this day. In Jesus' strong name I pray. **Amen.**

Questions for Reflection

1. What do you think of Perpetua's dilemma? Do you agree with her decision? Why or why not?

2. Does your commitment to Jesus Christ sometimes force you to make hard decisions? What resources do you draw on to help you make these kinds of decisions?

3. Have you ever had a sense that God was confirming the validity of a decision you made in faith? If so, how did this come about? What means did God use to give you a sense of assurance about your decision?

4. Why were Christians persecuted in the ancient world? Why and where are Christians persecuted today?

5. What role do moral examples (like Perpetua's) play in the development of a person's faith? What people influenced you as you developed Christian faith? Are you a positive example to others? If so, in what ways?

For Further Reading

"Sts. Felicitas and Perpetua," by J.P. Kirsch, in *The Catholic Encyclopedia*, found at http://www.newadvent.org/cathen/06029a.htm.

"Perpetua," by Rosemary Rader, in *A Lost Tradition: Women Writers of the Early Church*, by Patricia Wilson-Kastner, G. Ronald Kastner, Ann Millin, Rosemary Rader, and Jeremiah Reedy (University Press of America, 1981); pages 1–33. Offers the full text of Perpetua's diary.

"Perpetua and Felicitas," by David M. Scholer, in *Encyclopedia of Early Christianity*, edited by Everett Ferguson (Garland Publishing, Inc., 1990); page 712.
"Vibia Perpetua: A Martyr's Visions," in *Invitation to Christian Spirituality: An Ecumenical Anthology*, edited by John R. Tyson (Oxford University Press, 1999); pages 60–63. Offers a brief selection from Perpetua's writings.

Christians as the Romans Saw Them, by Robert Louis Wilken (Yale University Press, 2003).

Notes

[1] From "Perpetua," by Rosemary Rader, in *A Lost Tradition: Women Writers of the Early Church*, by Patricia Wilson-Kastner, G. Ronald Kastner, Ann Millin, Rosemary Rader, and Jeremiah Reedy (University Press of America, 1981); page 20.
[2] From "Perpetua," by Rosemary Rader, in *A Lost Tradition: Women Writers of the Early Church*; page 20.
[3] From "Perpetua," by Rosemary Rader, in *A Lost Tradition: Women Writers of the Early Church*; page 20.
[4] From "Perpetua," by Rosemary Rader, in *A Lost Tradition: Women Writers of the Early Church*; page 20.
[5] From "Perpetua," by Rosemary Rader, in *A Lost Tradition: Women Writers of the Early Church*; page 21.
[6] From "Perpetua," by Rosemary Rader, in *A Lost Tradition: Women Writers of the Early Church*; page 22.

[7] From "Perpetua," by Rosemary Rader, in *A Lost Tradition: Women Writers of the Early Church*; page 22.

[8] From "Perpetua," by Rosemary Rader, in *A Lost Tradition: Women Writers of the Early Church*; page 22.

[9] From "Perpetua," by Rosemary Rader, in *A Lost Tradition: Women Writers of the Early Church*; page 22.

[10] From "Perpetua," by Rosemary Rader, in *A Lost Tradition: Women Writers of the Early Church*; page 22.

[11] From "Perpetua," by Rosemary Rader, in *A Lost Tradition: Women Writers of the Early Church*; page 29.

[12] From "Perpetua," by Rosemary Rader, in *A Lost Tradition: Women Writers of the Early Church*; page 30.

[13] From http://www.quotationsbook.com/quote/4403.

II

Athanasius of Alexandria
(ca. 296–373)

Holy Persistence

I t is sometimes very difficult to see the long-term effects of short-term problems. Sometimes we get swept away in the tide of a "new" way of thinking and fail to stand up for what we know is right. Anthanasius was one of the few people in the fourth-century Christian church who recognized the serious implications of a "new" way of looking at Jesus' divinity. He struggled against what seemed to be impossible odds and personal acrimony in order to stand up for the truth about Jesus Christ as he understood it from Holy Scripture.

* * * *

The room was packed with Christian bishops, scholars, and other church leaders from all over the Mediterranean world. Over 1800 such persons had been invited to the first church council, at Nicaea (in Bithynia in northwest Asia Minor), in AD 325; and more than 300 agreed to attend. A steady hum was emitted by the crowd as church leaders and diplomats conferred with one another, waiting for the epic-making meeting to begin. Suddenly, those in the room fell into a rapt silence as the Roman emperor, Constantine the Great (ca. 280–337), strode confidently to the head of the gathering. He was wearing scarlet buskin boots and a vivid purple silk robe, which was decorated with gleaming precious stones; on his head was a crown.[1]

Constantine was the first Christian Roman emperor. He had converted to the Christian faith during his climb to imperial power. In 312, as he marched on Rome, he had a dramatic vision in which he saw the first two letters of "Christ" (in Greek), *chi rho*, emblazoned on the sun. He heard a voice from on high say to him, "In this you shall conquer." Obeying the words of God, Constantine ordered his troops to draw the *chi rho* on their shields; and they marched into battle against their enemies conscious of God's support. Constantine's army won a crushing victory that day at the Milvian bridge, and he eventually became the sole Roman emperor.[2]

In token of his victory, in 313 the new Emperor issued his famous "Edict of Milan," in which he put an end to the persecution of Christians and began to throw governmental support behind the Church. Constantine had given up the notion of imperial divinity, which previous emperors had used to unite the Romans under their rule. He had decided to be devout instead of divine. The Christian emperor would use the Christian faith as the glue to hold his far-flung empire together. He soon found, however, that the Christians were not as united among themselves as he needed them to be for his imperial strategy to work.

A serious debate had erupted in Alexandria, Egypt, in 319. The local bishop, a man named Alexander, had preached a sermon on the Trinity that at least one of his subordinates—a presbyter named Arius—thought was heretical. In claiming that the Father, Son, and Holy Spirit were all equally and eternally divine, it sounded to Arius (ca. 296–336) like Alexander was preaching that there were three gods. This caused Arius to begin researching and reconsidering the doctrine of the Trinity. His attention fastened on a phrase in John 1:18 that uses the word *monogenes* to describe how Jesus Christ, the Word, is God's "only begotten" Son (KJV). Arius reasoned, "If the Father begat the Son, he that was begotten had a beginning of existence; hence it is clear that there was [a time] when the Son was not."[3] From this analogy of a father begetting a son, Arius concluded that God the Father was eternal but the Son of God was not. This meant that the Son was not divine in the same way that the Father was divine. In effect, Arius had resolved the dilemma he saw in the doctrine of the Trinity by negating the deity of God the Son. His phrase, "There was a time when the Son was not," became a slogan for the new heresy, which robbed Jesus Christ of full divinity.

A small, dark man sat among the delegation from the Church of Alexandria. He was Athanasius (ca. 296–373), a deacon in the church and personal assistant to Bishop Alexander. He waited impatiently for the beginning of what he believed would be the debate of his life, and perhaps the most-important debate in the life of the church. Athanasius was devoted to the belief that Jesus was both God and man. In 318, at the tender age of nineteen, he wrote a treatise entitled *On the Incarnation of the Word of God*, in which he explained that the Incarnation ("The Word became flesh and lived among us" [John 1:14].) was the key to understanding both the person and the work of Jesus Christ. The logic of Athanasius, in this book, was devout and unassailable. In essence, he reasoned,

> The Bible teaches that only God can save.
> The Bible teaches that Jesus saves.
> Therefore, Jesus is God.

Athanasius further argued that Scripture urges people to worship Jesus and to pray in his name. This would be utter blasphemy unless Jesus was fully God, and the Bible would not urge its readers to commit blasphemy.

This understanding put Athanasius at odds with Arius because Athanasius argued as strenuously for the full deity of God the Son and for the full equality of God the Father and the Son as Arius argued against those beliefs. In Athanasius' view, the Incarnation and Christian redemption belonged together. Humans, who were made in the image of God (Genesis 1:26) and had fallen into sin, needed to be restored to God's image in order to enjoy salvation and life with God. This was the logic of the Incarnation: "The word of God came in His own Person, because it was He alone, the Image of the Father, Who could recreate man made after the Image."[4] So, as Athanasius argued in another place, Jesus, God's Son, became what we are to make us what he is.

To accomplish this redemption of humanity, death and corruption had to be defeated by the Son of God. Athanasius explained, "In order to effect this re-creation...He had first to do away with death and corruption. Therefore He assumed a human body, in order that in it death might once for all be destroyed, and that men might be renewed according to the Image [of God]. The Image of the Father only was sufficient for this need."[5] As if to witness to the divine identity of the Son of God, even the forces of nature broke their silence during the crucifixion of Jesus (Matthew 27:51-54; Luke 23:44-45). Athanasius wrote,

Even the very creation broke silence at His behest and, marvelous to relate, confessed with one voice before the cross, that monument to victory, that He Who suffered thereon in the body was not man only, but Son of God and Saviour of all. The sun veiled his face, the earth quaked, the mountains were rent asunder, all men were stricken with awe. These things showed that Christ on the cross was God, and that all creation was His slave and was bearing witness by its fear to the presence of its Master.[6]

To answer Athanasius' *On the Incarnation*, but by different media, Arius composed creeds, songs, and hymns that reflected his new theology. He popularized these not only in Alexandria, Egypt, but all across the eastern Mediterranean world. The debate quickly became extremely rancorous. Athanasius' opponents could not defeat his scripturally based arguments, so they called him "a black dwarf" in derision.[7]

Emperor Constantine had sent one of his most-trusted ministers to Egypt to try to forestall what seemed to be an impending schism in the church. When that effort failed, he resolved to settle the matter at a universal church council.

Constantine was a tall and vigorous man. One commentator reports that he had "fierce, lionlike eyes." [8] The gaze of all those assembled for the Council of Nicaea was riveted on him as he addressed them from his throne. "It was once my chief desire," he declared, "to enjoy the spectacle of your united presence; and now that this desire is fulfilled, I feel myself bound to render thanks to God the universal King, because, in addition to all his other benefits, he has granted me a blessing higher than all the rest, in permitting me to see you not only all assembled together, but all united in a common harmony of sentiment."[9]

After thanking God and his listeners for their assistance, the Christian emperor returned again to the dissension among the Christians:

As soon as I heard that intelligence which I had least expected to receive, I mean the news of your dissension, I judged it to be of no secondary importance, but with the earnest desire that a remedy for this evil also might be found through my means, I immediately sent to require your presence. And now I rejoice in beholding your assembly; but I feel that my desires will be most completely fulfilled when I can see you all united in one judgment....Delay not, then, dear friends: delay not, ye ministers of God, and faithful servants of him who is our common Lord and Saviour: begin from this moment to discard the causes of that disunion which has existed among you, and remove the perplexities of controversy by embracing the principles of peace.[10]

This was an ominous note on which to begin the council. Those in attendance had been warned that the Emperor would be satisfied with nothing short of Christian unity. After ceremoniously burning before the whole assembly all the petitions the various bishops had sent him privately, Constantine opened the conference. The debate soon became loud and disorderly. One ancient church historian reported it was "like a battle in the dark"[11] because everyone struck out wildly, and no one seemed to know what was going on. This was because the committed Arians and anti-Arians (Both these groups were relatively few in number.) felt the pressing need to win over the vast majority of delegates, who were uncommitted. Constantine acted both as moderator and as participant in the debate. He invited Arius to state his case, and he listened carefully as Arius presented his point of view. At the end of his oration, Arius broke into one of his songs, which was echoed by his devotees in the audience:

The uncreated God has made the Son
A beginning of things created,
And by adoption has God made the Son
Into an advancement of Himself,
Yet the Son's substance is
Removed from the substance of the Father:
The Son is not equal to the Father,
Nor does He share the same substance.
God is the all-wise Father,
And the Son is the teacher of His mysteries:
The members of the Holy Trinity
Share unequal glories.[12]

The anti-Arians put their hands over their ears so they would not have to hear such blasphemies, and some shrieked and ran from the room. Others were enraged, engaged in heated debate, and fired questions at Arius. He answered, generally, by chanting one of his hymns. As the Emperor brought the meeting back to order, he invited Athanasius to speak in opposition to Arius' view.

Unfortunately, the exact words that Athanasius spoke on this occasion have been lost to us. But, given the various accounts, we know that he conducted himself with a dignity that befitted the occasion and gave a reasoned explanation of the importance of the Incarnation, as well as of the full deity of the Son. It is likely that his logic that day followed the same pattern that had been laid out in his book *On the Incarnation of the Word of God*. He had strongly argued, for example, that the Son did not surrender his divinity when becoming human:

> The Word was not hedged in by His body, nor did His presence in the body prevent His being present elsewhere as well. When He moved His body He did not cease also to direct the universe by His mind and might.... His body was for Him not a limitation, but an instrument, so that He was both in it and in all things, and outside all things, resting in the Father alone. At one and the same time—this is the wonder—as Man He was living a human life, and as Word He was sustaining the life of the universe, and as Son He was in constant union with the Father.[13]

Athanasius pointedly attacked Arius' conclusion that "there was a time in which the Son was not" and that the Father and Son "share unequal glories." Athanasius' speech did not settle the Arian question that day. The debate went on and on. When the council discussed the relationship of the Father and the Son, the Arians would wink at each other and come up with special meanings for standard Christian affirmations. For example, when a bishop would say that Jesus Christ is the very image of God (Colossians 1:15), the Arians would say they could affirm that statement because all humans were created in God's image (Genesis 1:26). When a bishop argued that Jesus Christ is the Power of God, the Arians said they could agree with that: "Even the caterpillar and locust are called the power of God."[14] In short, the Arians were willing to agree that the Son was like the Father, but they refused to confess that the Father and the Son shared the same divine nature or essence. They refused to affirm that they were completely equal.

Athanasius' arguments and patient persistence laid the foundation for gaining a majority vote for his position. Eventually, Eusebius of Caesarea presented a creed that was in use in his church. Further debate raged on about whether the creed should affirm that the "Father and Son are of similar substance" or whether it should say, "The Father and the Son are of the same substance." Once again, the anti-Arians, led by Athanasius, argued for the full equality of God the Father and God the Son. They were able to win the support of the majority of the bishops, and of Emperor Constantine as well. An early form of the Nicene Creed was drafted, one that was profoundly anti-Arian; and it was signed by most, but not all, the bishops in attendance (Three or four refused to sign.).

After seven weeks of strenuous meetings, the Council of Nicaea sdjourned with a new church creed and a new sense of Christian harmony. Arius was exiled, and the Arian bishops were deposed. People were talking about Athanasius being the next Archbishop of Byzantium, the highest church office in the East. His "career path" seemed stable and assuredly set with an upward trajectory. Soon he succeeded his mentor, Alexander, as Bishop of Alexandria, in Egypt.

One would think that this should be the "happy ending" that this particular story deserves, but it is not. Arians did not take their defeat as an accomplished fact. They continued to work behind the scenes to undermine the established creed and Athanasius' position. When Constantine died, the bishop who baptized him on his death bed was an Arian. Two of Constantine's sons, who succeeded their father on the throne, were confessed Arians. Under their rule, it became politically expedient to become silent or to become Arian. Many bishops compromised their faith and the creed they signed in order to survive. But Athanasius did not. He was tried and persecuted many times on terrible charges trumped up by his ecclesiastical opponents. Once he was even charged with murder and was acquitted only when he produced the supposed "victim"—alive and well—at his own trial. Five separate times Athanasius was exiled from his beloved Alexandria.

In his repeated exiles Athanasius continued to labor tirelessly on behalf of the Nicene Creed. One of his contemporaries remarked that during those dark decades it seemed that Athanasius stood alone "against the world." These labors in foreign climates and desert regions took their toll on the aging man. He stood against popular opinion and against what was convenient, however, in order to affirm that Jesus Christ was and is both God and man. Finally, Athanasius was able to return home to Alexandria in 373, just before death claimed him.

Although Athanasius did not live to see the final victory over Arianism, which came in 381 when the Council of Constantinople reaffirmed the Nicene Creed and committed the church to enforce it, Athanasius' actions and writings show that he both anticipated and prepared the way for the victory that came after him. He refused to accept what looked like a defeat as the final result; he trusted God and kept on working. He was able to see the importance of what he was doing from the standpoint of its long-term effects and thereby retained both his hope and his persistence in the cause to which he had committed himself.

Athanasius' actions and writings show that he anticipated and prepared the way for the victory that came after him. His persistent and clear-sighted Christian faith paved the way for the consensus that was enshrined in the Nicene Creed. He refused to accept temporary defeat as a final result; he trusted God and kept on working. In so doing, Athanasius was able to see the current problem from the standpoint of its long-term effects. This gave him the impetus and persistence to keep on working despite the challenges he faced all along the path to a final victory. In this way, Athanasius stands as a beacon to us when we feel we are facing impossible challenges and persistent failures when defending a theological position that we know to be scriptural and true.

Would that we would be so grasped by the wonder and importance of the divine-human nature of our Lord Jesus Christ that we would, like Athanasius, be willing to spend our entire adult lives testifying to it and explaining it! But we each have our own daily challenges as well. God can give us the holy persistence to honor our responsibilities and our commitments even when they seem too heavy to bear and the road that lies ahead of us seems too long. The benediction by the apostle Paul in 1 Corinthians 15:58 describes well the holy persistence that was in Athanasius and that we would have for our own: "My beloved," Paul wrote, "be steadfast, immovable, always excelling in the work of the Lord, because you know that in the Lord your labor is not in vain."

Prayer

Lord Jesus Christ, I am humbled and challenged as I contemplate the truth of your divine-human nature; and yet I know that you truly are both "very God" and "very man." I thank you for people like Athanasius who have understood the importance of this truth and have stood firmly on it, risking their careers and even their lives for it. I ask you that you would give me some of the holy persistence that was in Athanasius! Grant that I would be so grasped by a vision of your truth that I am able to work for it all the days of my life. In Jesus' name I pray. **Amen.**

Questions for Reflection

1. How important is the Incarnation (John 1:14) to your own Christian faith?

2. Would you agree with Athanasius that the belief that Jesus was both fully human and fully divine is a Christian doctrine worth taking a stand for? In what situations can you imagine yourself needing to defend this doctrine?

3. Have you ever been in a situation in which you had to take an unpopular position because of your Christian faith? If so, did you experience alienation or estrangement from others for doing so?

4. Have you ever invested large amounts of faith and effort in a project only to have it produce ambiguous results? If so, what did you do? What should we do when we are in such a situation?

5. Have you ever had a moral or spiritual victory that felt a lot like a defeat? What did you do? Were you able to take the "long view" (instead of the short term) attitude toward that situation?

For Further Reading

On the Incarnation, by Athanasius (St Vladimir's Seminary Press, 1996).

The Life of the Blessed Emperor Constantine, by Eusebius; see http://www.fordham.edu/halsall/basis/vitaconstantine.html.

Champion of Truth: The Life of Saint Athanasius, by Michael Molloy (Alba House, 2003).

The Holy Fire: The Fathers of the Eastern Church, by Robert Payne (St Vladimir's Seminary Press, 1980); pages 67–112.

Notes

[1] From *The Holy Fire*, by Robert Payne (St Vladimir's Seminary Press, 1980); page 80.

[2] From *The Story of Christianity*, by Justo L. González, Vol. 1 (HarperSanFrancisco, 1984); page 173.

[3] From *Documents of the Christian Church*, edited by Henry Bettenson (Oxford University Press, 1963); page 40.

[4] From *On the Incarnation*, by Athanasius (St Vladimir's Seminary Press, 1996); page 41.

[5] From *On the Incarnation*; page 41.

[6] From *On the Incarnation*; page 48.

[7] From *The Story of Christianity*, Vol. 1; page 174.

[8] From *The Holy Fire*; page 81.

[9] From *Medieval Sourcebook: Eusebius of Caesarea: Life of Constantine*, by Eusebius; Book III, Chapter 12.

[10] From *Medieval Sourcebook: Eusebius of Caesarea: Life of Constantine*; Book III, Chapter 12.

[11] From *The Holy Fire*; page 82.

[12] From *The Holy Fire*; pages 82–83.

[13] From *On the Incarnation*; page 45.

[14] See http://www.archive.org/stream/athanasius01newmuoft/athanasius01newmuoft_djvu.txt.

III

Augustine of Hippo
(354–430)

The Human Heart Is Restless

L ate night snacks are one of my real enemies when it comes to trying to keep my girth and my weight under control. I know that it is
best to go to bed hungry, but sometimes I am so hungry for a particular food that I just cannot get it off my mind. Imagine dreaming of
pizza or Buffalo wings. How silly it seems to lie in bed, dead-tired, yet restless because I am hungry for something really "good."

The human heart has hungers of its own. Our hearts were created for
fellowship with God, who made us in his own image (Genesis 1:26). Living apart from God or living without a close relationship with God leaves
our hearts craving something more. We may have health and sustenance.
We may have all the accoutrements necessary for a comfortable life; but
deep inside we are hungry for something more, something really "good."

The narrative that follows describes one of Christendom's most-famous
"hungry hearts," that of Augustine. Looking at his life-pilgrimage will
almost certainly remind us about something of our own: It will remind us
how restless the human heart is until it finds rest in God.

* * * *

Augustine was born in Tagaste, North Africa. His mother was a native
North African (a Berber), and his father was a minor Roman official.
Augustine's mother, Monica, was a devout Christian. His father was an

equally zealous pagan. Augustine would later remark that he had imbibed his Christianity "with his mother's milk."[1]

As Augustine began to grow into adolescence, his father saw to it that he experienced the pleasures of paganism. At seventeen, young Augustine left home to study philosophy and rhetoric at the university in nearby Carthage; and he left his Christian faith behind as well. He became involved in a cult called Manicheism, in part because it promised him easy answers to the complex problems of human life and in part because it did not make the kind of moral demands on him that Christianity did. He pursued sensuality in its various forms and became a sexual libertine. He wrote in his book *Confessions*, "Bodily desire, like a morass, and adolescent sex welling up within me exuded mists which clouded over and obscured my heart, so that I could not distinguish the clear light of true love from the murk of lust. Love and lust together seethed within me. In my tender youth they swept me away over the precipice of my body's appetites and plunged me in the whirlpool of sin."[2]

As Augustine pursued his studies, he pursued (with greater ardor) pleasure as well. He found himself becoming more and more drawn to sensuality. He lived with a mistress for more than fifteen years, and she eventually bore him a son; yet this relationship did not satisfy him. Over time, his perfunctory religious duties also seemed to be utterly meaningless. His heart was hungry for something—something more than what he could find in sensuality. This heart-hunger set his feet on a path that would lead to a long spiritual pilgrimage; and like the prodigal son in Jesus' parable (Luke 15), it would be a long road "home."

An intelligent and reflective person, Augustine tried to make sense of his life throughout this pilgrimage. He left us a detailed examination of his search for meaning in the form of his spiritual autobiography entitled *Confessions* (ca. 398). The word *confessions* reminds us of the lurid details reported by supermarket tabloids, but Augustine meant the term differently. In one of his sermons he explained that for him confession was related to the "accusation of oneself and the praise of God." In this sense, then, *Confessions* amounts to an extremely honest examination of his conscience, which is set in the form of a prayer or extended conversation with God. The book is remarkable not only for the brutal honesty with which Augustine addresses his feelings and his shortcomings but also for the way in which he invites his readers into the process of thinking through the question, What is the meaning of life?

In reflecting on this process, Augustine discovered that the human heart is restless, forever restless, until it finds rest in God. He asked,

Can any praise be worthy of the Lord's majesty? [Ps. 145:3]...Man is one of your creatures, Lord, and his instinct is to praise you. He bears about him the mark of death, the sign of his own sin, to remind him that you *thwart the proud* [1 Pet. 5:5]. But still, since he is a part of your creation, he wishes to praise you. The thought of you stirs him so deeply that he cannot be content unless he praises you, because you made us for yourself and our hearts find no peace until they rest in you.[3]

As Augustine found, however, human sin alienates us from God, our true source of identity and meaning, and bids us to find meaning elsewhere. In describing the attractiveness of human sin, Augustine's attention turned in an unlikely direction: to the theft of a large quantity of pears that he and other young hoodlums stole from a neighbor's tree:

If the crime of theft which I committed that night as a boy of sixteen were a living thing, I could speak to it and ask what was that, to my shame, I loved in it. I had no beauty because it was a robbery. It is true that the pears which we stole had beauty, because they were created by you, the good God....But it was not the pears that my unhappy soul desired. I had plenty of my own, better than those, and I only picked them so that I might steal. For no sooner had I picked them than I threw them away, and tasted nothing in them but my own sin, which I relished and enjoyed. If any part of one of those pears passed my lips, it was the sin that gave it flavour."[4]

Considering the spiritual state that was reflected by this wanton act of disobedience, which was carried out simply for the "rush" of freedom and the joy of disobedience, Augustine felt that he was getting close to the basis of the human dilemma. "Can anyone unravel this twisted tangle of knots?" he asked.[5]

In the year 383, Augustine left Carthage and relocated to Rome. After teaching rhetoric (public speaking and persuasion) for several years, he had become dissatisfied with provincial, little Carthage and longed to see the great capital of the Empire. He had become disenchanted with his unruly students and hoped to find better pupils and better philosophy in Rome. Once again he was disillusioned; his Roman students were both apathetic and dishonest. "They were quite unscrupulous," he wrote, "and justice meant nothing to them compared with the love of money."[6] Indeed, they skipped out without paying their tuition!

Through Manichean friends, Augustine was able to meet the prefect (mayor) of the city of Rome, a man named Symmachus. Through Symmachus, Augustine secured an appointment as the professor of rhetoric for the imperial court in Milan in 384. This was an extremely high position for a person who had just reached thirty years of age.

During this period of time, and even before Augustine left Carthage, he was beginning to become disillusioned with Manicheism. In Carthage, he had a disappointing meeting with Faustus, a bishop of the Manichees, who was reputed to be a great and knowledgeable theologian among them. Augustine recalled, "As soon as it became clear to me that Faustus was quite uninformed about the subjects in which I had expected him to be an expert, I began to lose hope that he could lift the veil and resolve the problems which perplexed me."[7]

When Augustine looked back on this period of his life, he recalled praying, "'Give me chastity and continence, but not yet.' For I was afraid that you [God] would answer my prayer at once and cure me too soon of the disease of lust, which I wanted satisfied, not quelled. I had wandered along the road of vice in the sacrilegious superstition of the Manichees, not because I thought it was right, but because I preferred it to the Christian belief, which I did not explore as I ought but opposed out of malice."[8]

Augustine's mother soon followed him to Milan, and she prevailed on him to accompany her to church. There he met the famous Christian bishop Ambrose, who would be an instrument used by God to bring Augustine into relationship with him. Looking back on that event, Augustine wrote, "Unknown to me, it was You [God] who led me to [Ambrose], so that I might knowingly be led by him to You. This man of God received me like a father, and as bishop, told me how glad he was that I had come."[9] The comparison between Ambrose and his teaching and Faustus was glaring: "There could be no comparison between the two. Faustus had lost his way among the fallacies of Manicheism, while Ambrose most surely taught the doctrine of salvation. But though *your mercy is unknown to sinners* [Ps. 119:155], such as I was then, . . . step by step, unwittingly, I was coming closer to it."[10] God's providence, Augustine concluded, had brought this Christian man into his life.

Augustine's road to faith was a long and circuitous one, however. While listening to Ambrose, he began to read Neoplatonic philosophy; and this proved to be more adequate than Manicheism. It seemed to pave the way for his understanding of the Bible, which Ambrose and his mother encouraged him to read. But still Augustine hung back. Sin held him like a slumber: "In the same way I was quite sure that it was better for me to give myself up to follow your [God's] love than surrender to my own lust. But while I wanted to follow the first course and was convinced that it was right, I was still a slave to the pleasures of the second. I had no answer to make when you said *Awake, you who sleep, and arise from the dead, and Christ shall give you light* [Eph. 5:14]."[11]

In a tumultuous and divided state of heart, Augustine sat down in the garden of the house where he lived. "My inner self was a house divided against itself,"[12] he recalled. Turning his back on sensuality and giving his life to Christ seemed like a simple act of will, but he could not will it wholeheartedly: "To will it was to do it. Yet I did not do it."[13] Augustine was riddled by doubt and "double-mindedness" (James 1:8), even in his prayers. "I kept saying, 'Let it be now, let it be now!' and merely by saying this I was on the point of making the resolution, I was on the point of making it, but I did not succeed."[14]

As Augustine searched his heart to ascertain what was holding him back from taking the step of faith, he heard the sing-song voice of a child repeating the refrain, "Take it and read, take it and read." Looking about and seeing no children and recalling no game in which such words would be chanted or sung, he decided to take it to be a divine command. He reached out and picked up the Bible that lay nearby. He recently had read the life of Saint Antony of the desert and recalled how the great saint had heard the voice of God in the words of Scripture being read as he walked past a church. So Augustine reached down and picked up the Bible, which he had been reading.

> I seized it and opened it, and in silence I read the first passage on which my eyes fell: *Not in reveling and drunkenness, not in lust and wantonness, not in quarrels and rivalries. Rather, arm yourselves with the Lord Jesus Christ; spend no more thought on nature and nature's appetites* [Rom. 13:13, 14]. I had no wish to read more and no need to do so. For in an instant, as I came to the end of the sentence, it was as though the light of confidence flooded into my heart and all the darkness of doubt was dispelled.[15]

This event was a tremendous turning point in Augustine's life. He told his mother and his Christian friends what had happened, and they all rejoiced. Augustine repeatedly spoke with Bishop Ambrose about his new-found faith and asked what books of the Bible he should be reading in order to gain Christian maturity. In addition to the Gospels and Epistles, Ambrose recommended Psalms—the prayer book of the ancient church. Augustine soon prayed in the words of Psalm 116:16, 17,

> Lord I am your servant, born of your own handmaid. You have broken the chains that bound me; I will sacrifice in your honour [Ps. 116:16-17]. Let me praise You in my heart, let me praise you with my tongue. . . .
>
> Who am I? What kind of man am I? What evil have I not done? Or if there is evil that I have not done, what evil is there that I have not spoken? If there is any that I have not spoken, what evil is there that I have not willed to do? But You, O Lord, are good. You are merciful. You saw how deep I was sunk in death, and it was your power that drained dry the well of corruption in the depths of my heart. And all that you asked of me was to deny my own will and accept yours.[16]

In 387, Augustine and his son were baptized as Christians by Ambrose of Milan. By 388, Augustine was on his way back to North Africa to serve Christ and the church there. Returning to Tagaste, he established a monastic community among Christian friends. In 391, he had entered the Christian ministry, as a priest. Augustine was a very able pastor and preacher—as indicated by the more than 350 authentic sermons of his which have survived from antiquity. By 396, he was named coadjutor (assistant) bishop of the city of Hippo; and he soon succeeded to the role of bishop. He held this position until his death in 430.

Augustine adorned the office of bishop with great vigor and dedication, guiding the church through dangerous heresies (such as Manicheism and Pelagianism) and potential schisms (the Donatist controversy). During the same period he published many important theological works, including Confessions, The City of God, and On the Trinity—any one of which would have been considered important enough to cause him to rank among the leading Christian theologians of all time.

Like the prodigal of Jesus' parable (Luke 15), Augustine found his way back to his Father's house. There he found what his heart was hungry for. Indeed, in retrospect, he was able to see that God had been actively seeking him all the time that he was wandering restlessly from one superficial attachment to another. Augustine's newfound relationship with God filled his life with meaning and purpose. It gave him the heartfelt love he had sought, mistakenly, in so many sensual relationships. The sense of acceptance and belonging that came with this realization empowered Augustine's long life. By faith, Augustine became what God had created him to be: God's own unique person, God's own child.

Prayer

Dear God, I thank you that you have made me, made me for yourself. You know what is in me—both for good and for ill—and yet you love me as your own child. I confess that my heart is sometimes restless, causing me to wander from your will and ways. I ask that you would heal my heart and make it wholly yours. I pray that you will not only forgive my wanderings, but that you will help me be so transformed by your love that I will not wander again. Teach me to love the things you love. Teach me to be the person you would have me be. In Jesus' name I pray. **Amen.**

Questions for Reflection

1. What is your heart hungry for?

2. What distractions keep modern people from giving themselves wholeheartedly to God?

3. What things cause you to feel "divided" between your secular life and your spiritual life?

4. What role do the Bible and Christian relationships play in your faith pilgrimage?

5. Have you ever felt that God was speaking directly to you through the Scriptures? through Christian worship? If so, what did you do?

For Further Reading

Augustine of Hippo: Selected Writings, edited by Mary Clark (Paulist Press, 1984).

Augustine of Hippo, by Peter Brown (University of California Press, 1969.

Saint Augustine's Confessions, translated by R.S. Pine-Coffin (Penguin Books, 1961).

Notes

[1] See *Saint Augustine: Confessions*, translated by R.S. Pine-Coffin (Penguin Books, 1961); III:4:59.
[2] From *Confessions*; II:1:43.
[3] From *Confessions*; I:1:21.
[4] From *Confessions*; II:6:49.
[5] From *Confessions*; II:10:52.
[6] From *Confessions*; V:12:106.
[7] From *Confessions*; V:7:98.
[8] From *Confessions*; VII:7:169.
[9] From *Confessions*; V:13:107.
[10] From *Confessions*; V:13:107.
[11] From *Confessions*; VIII:5:165.
[12] From *Confessions*; VIII:8:170.
[13] From *Confessions*; VIII:8:171.
[14] From *Confessions*; VIII:11:175.
[15] From *Confessions*; VIII:8:178.
[16] From *Confessions*; IX:1:181.

IV

Anselm of Canterbury

(1033–1109)

Faith Seeking Understanding

Sometimes it seems that the life of faith is like a walk into the dark. We keep groping our way ahead without clearly seeing where we are going. Our heads and our hearts seem to be out of sync, and the pieces of our lives do not fit together. Anselm knew what this situation was like. He had a deep-seated faith, as well as a passion to understand as much as he could about God and faith. He learned that faith can lead directly to greater understanding if the knowledge of God is sought prayerfully and relentlessly. Anselm had the insight to see that Christian theology is not merely knowledge about God. Christian theology is knowing God in a way that is rooted in personal experience and relationship, that is satisfying in the inner person. In particular, Anselm wanted to understand the mystery of the incarnation of Jesus Christ: "Why Did God Become a Man?" he asked in the title of his most famous book.

* * * *

Anselm was born in Aosta, located in northern Italy. Aosta was a region of unsurpassed beauty, with fertile valleys painted against the background of Alpine vistas. Anselm came to faith at an early age; and by the time he was fifteen, he was intent on entering the monastic life. His father refused to give him permission to do so, however.

Anselm's mother died soon thereafter, and his father's temper and harsh attitudes made life in his home unbearable. In 1059, Anselm crossed the Alps and traveled throughout France. He soon found himself drawn to the Abbey of Bec, in Normandy, where the famous monk and theologian Lanfranc was abbot. Anselm offered himself as a novice at the Abbey of Bec in 1060 and was received into a life of prayer, study, and service based on Benedict's Rule. Within three years, Lanfranc was made abbot of the monastery of Caen. Anselm was elected to replace him as abbot at Bec. He spent the next fifteen years as abbot, living a life of study, teaching, preaching, and prayer.

Anselm was a great Christian thinker, but he was a thinker who bathed his intellectual inquiries in prayer. For him, prayer and meditation on God's truth was the force behind theological inquiry. One of his prayers from this period of time reflects his mood:

> God of truth,
> I ask that I may receive,
> so that my joy may be full.
> Meanwhile, let my mind meditate on it,
> let my tongue speak of it,
> let my heart love it,
> let my mouth preach it,
> my flesh thirst for it,
> and my whole being desire it,
> until I enter into the joy of my Lord,
> who is God one and triune, blessed forever, Amen.[1]

During his work as abbot, Anselm had responsibility for teaching his fellow monks and novices. Eadmer, who was Anselm's friend and earliest biographer, remembered that he made his teachings live in the hearts and minds of his students by telling them folksy stories about faith. Anselm also began to write theological works that would become internationally famous in his own time and remain so today.

Two of these influential works were *Monologian* (ca. 1078) and *Proslogian* (ca. 1079). Written while Anselm was serving at Bec, they amount to reverential inquiries into the existence of God. Traditionally, they have been called "proofs" for the existence of God; but they are more reminders than "proofs" in the modern sense of the word. Through prayer and prayerful reflection, Anselm hoped he could help his readers believe in God with more certainty. In the famous preface to *Proslogian*, Anselm wrote,

> I acknowledge, O Lord, with thanksgiving, that thou hast created this thy image in me, so that, remembering thee, I may think of thee, may love thee. But this image is so effaced and worn away by my faults, it is so obscured by the smoke of my sins, that it cannot do what it was made to do, unless you renew and reform it. I am not trying, O Lord, to penetrate thy loftiness, for I cannot begin to match my understanding with it, but I desire in some measure to understand thy truth, which my heart believes and loves. For I do not seek to understand in order to believe, but I believe in order to understand. For this too I believe, that "unless I believe, I shall not understand" [Is. 7:9].[2]

As a scholar in the tradition of Augustine, Anselm believed that human sin tainted the image of God in which all humans had been created (Genesis 1:26); hence, he prayed to God to enlighten his understanding and reform his inner nature so that he could understand God more adequately. He prayed in his meditation entitled "The Mind Aroused to Contemplate God,"

> Look on me, O Lord, and hear me, and enlighten me and show me Thyself. Restore Thyself to me, that it may be well with me; Thou, without whom it goes ill with me. Direct, O Lord, my labours and my endeavours unto Thee, for without Thee I am nothing worth. Thou invitest me; help me, O Lord, I pray Thee, that I sigh not from despair, but breathe again and hope. O Lord, I pray Thee, for it is soured by its lonesomeness, sweeten my heart with Thy consolations. O Lord, I pray Thee, for I have begun to seek Thee hungering, let me not go away empty; I have drawn near famished with want, let me not depart unsatisfied.[3]

In *Monologian*, Anselm looked to the physical structures of our world. He believed that the order, beauty, movement, purpose, and design he saw at work in the world should cause the reverent observer to think of our God as the source of these things. In this he was taking seriously the witness of passages like Psalm 19:1-4:

> The heavens are telling the glory of God;
>   and the firmament proclaims his handiwork.
> Day to day pours forth speech,
>   and night to night declares knowledge.

From the design of the universe, Anselm postulated a Divine Designer. From the sense of purpose that most humans feel at work in their lives, Anselm pointed to the One who gives life its meaning and purpose. In *Proslogian*, Anselm sought to simplify his many arguments for the existence of God into one basic point that was so solid it could not, reasonably, be doubted. In reflecting on this task, his attention was drawn to the words of Psalm 14:1, "Fools say in their hearts, 'There is no God.'" Anselm took this assertion to mean that the existence of God must be so self-evident that it is foolish to doubt it.

But in what sense could this be true? Well, one thing that "fools" were certain of was the fact that they doubted God's existence. Yet even the process of doubting God's existence involves an awareness of the idea of God. And where did humans get the idea of God? It came from God, which of course implied God's existence. So the "fools" of Psalm 14 are not mean-spirited doubters. Doubters are foolish simply because they do not realize that in the process of doubting they have proved the existence of God. Anselm put it this way: "Even the fool, then, must be convinced that a being than which none greater can be thought exists at least in his understanding, since when he hears this he understands it, and whatever is understood is in the understanding."[4]

Anselm's fifteen years of teaching, study, and prayer probably passed by rapidly. No doubt it was a time to which he often looked back wistfully as he became enmeshed in the political struggles of nearby England.

In 1093, the ailing William II, King of England, appointed Anselm to the position of Archbishop of Canterbury. The post had been vacant for over a year; but fearing his death may have been at hand, King William II appointed Anselm to the position as part of his attempt to make amends for his sins. Somewhat naively, Anselm received the "pallium" (the white woolen stole that was the emblem of his office) from the hands of William II. Church law specified that the pallium must have been blessed by the reigning pope and that the rightful archbishop would be the one installed by the church and not by the king. There was some question, however, about who was the rightful pope.

Urban II was pope in Rome; and an anti-pope, Clement III, reigned in France. William II, King of England, used this confusion over papal authority as an opportunity to seize control of ecclesiastical matters in England. This put Anselm squarely on the front lines of an ongoing struggle between the church and the monarchy of England over who had the right to appoint church leaders in England. This controversy is called the "investiture struggle" because it had to do with the right of investing a person with ecclesiastical office. Both the king and the pope wanted authority over the Archbishop of Canterbury, and Anselm's sympathies in this matter were with Pope Urban II.

In the midst of the investiture struggle (1094–1098), Anselm wrote what would become his most-famous work. Once again his faith was seeking understanding. This time he found himself drawn to the question of the incarnation of our Lord Jesus Christ. In the title of this treatise Anselm asked pointedly, *Cur Deos Homo?* ("Why Did God Become Man?").

Anselm addressed this question, in part, because of the prevalence of the so-called "ransom to the devil theory" in his own day. Many people, including the saintly Bernard of Clairvaux, argued that Christ died to pay a ransom to the devil and thereby to set humankind free from the debt of sin and death that the devil holds over people. Anselm found this theology appalling because of the unscriptural authority it seemed to give Satan over human lives. A strong believer in original sin, Anselm thought that human choice was the basis of the devil's hold over us, not some sort of primordial debt. The "ransom theory" had the danger of giving rise to a "devil-made-me-do-it" theology that seemed to absolve humans from full responsibility for doing evil.

Anselm approached the question "Why Did God Become Man?" by focusing his (and our) attention on the saving work of Christ. At one point he said, in effect, "Christ became what we are, to make us into what He is." The gist of Anselm's argument is couched in the language of castles and chivalry, that is to say, the language of his own times; but the logic is timeless.

As we look into his argument for the Atonement (the saving death of Jesus Christ), we must examine two terms. The first of these is "debt," and the second is "satisfaction." Debt is something that most of us know about through such things as our mortgage, credit cards, or educational loans. Anselm was concerned about a debt of *honor*, however. Honor was a tremendously important matter in medieval society. Serfs swore loyalty to the lord of the manor, and the lord of the manor swore to protect them. People swore oaths of honor to their trade, their city, their nation, their military group, and so forth. This relationship of honor became Anselm's metaphor for the divine-human relationship. The second concept, "satisfaction," is also used in a technical way; it does not follow the modern, dictionary definition: "to gratify one's desires." Satisfaction, in Anselm's vocabulary, describes the process whereby a debt is properly discharged. While the logic of the book *Cur Deos Homo?* can be summarized by saying that Christ became human in order to make humans what he is, the basic argument is slightly more complicated than that. But it can be summarized in nine logical steps:

> (1) Every creature owes a debt of honor and obedience to God the Creator.
> (2) Human sin is disobedience and a nonpayment of this debt.
> (3) Justice demands that the sinner make satisfaction for his or her debt.
> (4) Punishment is the suitable satisfaction, and punishment must equal the debt owed.
> (5) Humans are utterly powerless to make satisfaction for such a large debt.
> (6) The debt is owed by a human; therefore a human *ought* to pay it.
> (7) But the debt is so large that only God *could* pay it.
> (8) In his wisdom and mercy, God sent the God-Man, Jesus Christ, to pay the debt owed by humanity.
> (9) The life of Christ is more than adequate as a payment for our sins. [5]

Anselm's argument is not perfect, in that it characterizes the divine-human relationship in a somewhat mechanical way. But it does a good job of penetrating some of the inner logic of the Incarnation. In the tension between a debt that "ought" to be paid by humans and the realization that this debt is so huge that it could not be paid by a human lay something of the truth of divine grace. In the cross of Jesus Christ, God was reconciling the world unto himself; God was doing something for us that we could not do for ourselves. As the apostle Paul wrote, "In Christ God was reconciling the world to himself, not counting their trespasses against them, and entrusting the message of reconciliation to us" (2 Corinthians 5:19). As Anselm exclaimed, "What greater mercy could be imagined, than for God the Father to say to the sinner, condemned to eternal torments, and without any power of redeeming himself from them, 'Receive my only-begotten Son, and give him for yourself,' and for the Son himself to say, 'Take me, and redeem yourself'? For they as much as say this when they call us and draw us to the Christian faith."[6]

Anselm's constancy in claiming ecclesiastical rights in the investiture struggle soon caused him to run afoul of King William II, and Anselm was forced to spend the years 1097–1100 in exile. When William died in 1100, he was succeeded on the throne by Henry I, who invited Anselm to return. Once again the question of Anselm's pallium became a point of contention, however. As a result, he spent 1103–1106 in exile and was not able to return to Canterbury until 1106, where he finished his illustrious career and life in 1109.

In the life and thought of Anselm of Canterbury, we see that the life of the heart and the life of the mind can fit together harmoniously and energize each other. His faith, which relentlessly sought understanding, was a tremendous comfort to Anselm; and it gave him great courage and great insight into the things of God. We can certainly be grateful that Anselm had such penetrating insight into the two natures of our Lord, Jesus Christ. Faith's assertion of the identity of Jesus as the God-Man reached satisfying explanation in Anselm's hands. How wonderful that the answer to Anselm's thought-provoking question "Why Did God Become Man?" is simply, clearly, and emphatically answered: "for my salvation, for the salvation of the whole world." Anselm had the insight to see that Christian theology is not merely knowledge about God. Christian theology is knowledge of God that is rooted in experience and relationship and is satisfying in the inner person.

Prayer

Gracious God, thank you for creating me as a whole person. Thank you that I have a heart and a mind, and thank you for giving me a life that marries my heart and mind in faithful devotion to you. Thank you for the gift of faith! Yet I say in the words of the Gospel, "I believe; help my unbelief!" (Mark 9:24). Help me prayerfully to pursue an intellectually satisfying understanding of you that goes hand-in-hand with the life of faith. Help me see doubt and confusion not as impediments to my faith, but as opportunities for its growth and understanding. Give me the Light of life so that I might not walk in darkness and may not stumble. Give me the kind of passion that Anselm had for knowing and following Jesus, the God-Man! In his name I pray. **Amen.**

Questions for Reflection

1. Does "faith seeking understanding" describe your understanding of the relationship of faith and reason? Why or why not?

2. Do you agree with Anselm that looking at nature and the physical world can give a person evidence of God's existence and nature? Why or why not?

3. Have you ever experienced the presence of God in a special way through viewing the wonders of nature?

4. Do you agree with Anselm's criticism of the view that the devil holds Christians in bondage and makes them do things against their will?

5. How do you think of the relationship between the incarnation of Jesus Christ ("the Word became flesh") and Jesus' saving death? What are the strengths of Anselm's explanation? What are the weaknesses?

For Further Reading

Anselm, by G.R. Evans (Morehouse Publishing, 1989).

A Scholastic Miscellany: Anselm to Ockham, edited and translated by Eugene Fairweather (The Macmillan Company, 1970); pages 69–210.

Anselm's Prayers and Meditations of Saint Anselm With The Proslogian, edited by Bendicta Ward (Penguin, 1973).

Notes

[1] From *The Prayers and Meditations of Saint Anselm With The Proslogian*, edited by Benedicta Ward (Penguin Books, 1973); page 81.
[2] From *A Scholastic Miscellany: Anselm to Ockham*, edited and translated by Eugene R. Fairweather (The Macmillan Company, 1970); page 73.
[3] From *St. Anselm's Book of Meditations and Prayers*, M.R. translation (Burns and Oats, 1872); page 286.
[4] From "A Proof for the Existence of God," in *Readings in Christian Thought*, Second Edition, edited by Hugh T. Kerr (Abingdon, 1990); page 84.
[5] From "Christ's Atonement for Sin," in *Readings in Christian Thought*; pages 85–93.
[6] From "Christ's Atonement for Sin," in *Readings in Christian Thought*; pages 92–93.

V

Francis and Clare of Assisi
(ca. 1181–1254)

Holy Poverty

Poverty and wealth stand in stark contrast in our modern world. Poverty is a source of profound human suffering. It causes illness, crime, and various forms of social disintegration. This was also the case in the twelfth century. Indeed, the affluence of a few privileged people seemed to contribute directly to the impoverishment of many. The fortunate few who were able pursued the acquisition of wealth and goods with the kind of determination that suggested that materialism and not Christian faith shaped the habits of their hearts and lives. If this scenario sounds at all familiar, then you have an immediate understanding of both the relevancy and the challenge of Francis and Clare of Assisi. Upon coming to robust Christian faith, they found themselves scandalized by the materialism and the poverty of their age; and they resolved to try to do something about it.

* * * *

Francis was born Giovanni de Bernadone in 1181 in the town of Assisi in north-central Italy. He was the son of a wealthy cloth merchant, Pietro de Bernadone, whose business often took him to the south of France. On one of his business trips to France, Pietro met and fell in love with a beautiful young woman named Pica; she eventually returned to Assisi with him as his wife. Pietro was also away from Assisi on business when his son

Giovanni was born and christened. When Pietro heard that he had a son, he was overjoyed. He also insisted that the boy's name be changed from Giovanni to Francesco (Francis) in honor of the beautiful homeland of his mother. There was a flair for the romantic in Pietro's heart!

Francis grew up in a bilingual household; at an early age he learned to speak his father's Italian and his mother's French. He also learned Latin and grammar from the parish priest in the local school. Francis had the good fortune of being born in a region that was full of natural beauty, and he developed an appreciation for the beauty of nature that would stay with him throughout his life. He had no further education than that which was afforded by the parish school, but he did not need a university degree to embark on the career that was chosen for him: Francis was expected to enter his father's lucrative mercantile business.

Unfortunately, Francis did not have the sort of business sense that had been given to Pietro. In fact, Francis seemed more adept at spending money than he was at making it; and in this respect he was a disappointment to his father. Francis was wonderfully popular in Assisi, however. He was one of the richest boys in town, and he had enormous talents when it came to having a good time. He was fair of face and full of mirth. He and his friends often toured town singing the songs of the traveling troubadours, stopping now and then for a drink at their favorite taverns. In these endeavors Francis sometimes donned the multicolored uniform of a court jester and led the crowds in drunken choruses.

The times in which Francis lived were full of stark contrasts. Feudalism still held a large portion of Europe in its oppressive grip. In the old agrarian economy, many people were so bound to the land by custom and poverty that they lived as virtual slaves. But here and there, as in the Italian trading cities, a new economy was emerging. International trade was causing an influx of new wealth, and this wealth had a dizzying effect on people because of the great poverty that both preceded and surrounded it.

The Church of Francis' day was the single-largest landowner in Europe. Hence, the Church employed legions of serfs to work the fields and hired armies to protect them.

Illiteracy bred superstition, and these two formed the warp and woof of popular piety. The fascination with holy relics and the bones of the saints was a significant aspect of the piety of the times.

Most of the mystery and theology that came into the stooped-over-life of working people flowed through the practical life of the Church and the sacraments. The great cathedrals were like textbooks for the illiterate. The ornate windows, statues, tapestries, music, and liturgy enabled people to see and act out the mysteries of Christian faith and forgiveness, whether they fully understood them or not.

There already had been several strong reactions against the state of affairs in the medieval Roman Catholic Church, and two of the most-famous ones (by the Waldensians and Cathars) sprang from the region that was home to Francis and his parents. It seemed to be a hothouse for religious reaction against the excesses of the Church. We know from the statements of some of its own leaders that the Church in that region was unusually corrupt and materialistic. Some of the local priests were illiterate, indolent, and profane. Simony (the buying or selling of ecclesiastical pardons, offices, or employment) and keeping concubines had become common practices among the clergy. In some places the Church had begun to forfeit the respect of earnest souls.

In 1202, the city of Assisi went to war against nearby Perugia. Francis, along with many of his friends and neighbors, served in this war. Unfortunately, Francis was no better at soldiering than he had been at business; and he wound up spending a very reflective year as a prisoner of war. In 1204, he found himself in the army again, this time in the service of Pope Innocent III.

Disease took Francis prisoner this time. As he lay on his cot with a high fever raging, Francis heard a voice asking him, "Why do you desert the Lord for the servant, the Prince for his vassal?"

"My Lord," Francis asked, "what do you want me to do?"

The voice answered, "Go back to your home; there you will be told what you are to do."[1]

Francis left the army immediately and returned to Assisi. He found himself even less interested in the family business than he had been before and, surprisingly, much more interested in religion. He began to take long walks through the countryside, communing with God through nature. Near Assisi he found the dilapidated chapel of San Damiano, and it became one of his favorite places for prayer. While Francis was praying there one day in February 1207, he believed that he heard Christ speaking to him from the cross on the altar. The voice assured Francis that Christ had accepted his life and soul as a dedication to the risen Lord. Bonaventure, in his *Life of St. Francis*, described the scene this way:

One day when Francis went out to meditate in the fields, he walked beside the church of San Damiano which was threatening to collapse because of extreme age. Inspired by the Spirit, he went inside to pray. Prostrate before the image of the Crucified, he was filled with consolation as he prayed. While his tear-filled eyes were gazing at the Lord's cross, he heard with his bodily ears a voice coming from the cross, telling him three times: Francis, go and repair my house, which you see, is falling completely into ruin."[2]

Francis was amazed at the sound of the voice, since he was alone in the church. Hearing this voice was a transforming experience for him. Francis knew in his heart that these had been God's words to him, and he quickly set about to obey them. He hurried to a nearby town and sold everything he had with him and brought the money back to the chapel at San Damiano. Finding the priest there, Francis asked him to accept the money and use it for the repair of the chapel; he also asked if he might stay with him for a short time. The priest agreed to allow Francis to stay and work at San Damiano for a short time, but he refused to accept the money Francis offered for fear of the disapproval of the young man's parents. "True despiser of money that he was," Bonaventure wrote, "Francis threw it on a window sill, valuing it no more than if it were dust."[3] Francis subsequently wrote his "Prayer Before the Crucifix" which hearkens back to the events of that momentous day:

> Most high,
> glorious God,
> enlighten the darkness of my heart
> and give me, Lord
> a correct faith,
> a certain hope
> a perfect charity,
> sense and knowledge
> so that I may carry out Your holy and true command.[4]

From that day onward Francis dedicated himself to living a Christlike life.

Another day as he walked through the countryside, Francis met a man with leprosy. The man was so disfigured by the disease that Francis turned away in revulsion. Rebuking himself for an act that was not worthy of Jesus Christ, Francis returned to the man and emptied his purse into the leper's hand. He then kissed the disease-ridden hand. This act, Francis would subsequently explain, marked a revolution in his spiritual life. Thereafter he frequently visited the hovels of the lepers, bringing them alms, blessings, and spiritual comfort.

In February 1209, as he was hearing mass in a local church, Francis was struck by the words of the morning lesson as the priest read them from the Holy Scripture. They were the words of Jesus to his apostles: "As you go, proclaim the good news, 'The kingdom of heaven has come near.' Cure the sick, raise the dead, cleanse the lepers, cast out demons. You received without payment; give without payment. Take no gold, or silver, or copper in your belts, no bag for your journey, or two tunics, or sandals, or a staff" (Matthew 10:7-10). It seemed to Francis that these words had come directly from Jesus Christ to him personally, and he resolved to obey these words as a command from the Lord. Thus, Bonaventure reports, "This lover of apostolic poverty was then filled with an indescribable joy and said: 'This is what I want; this is what I long for with all my heart.'"[5]

Francis resolved to preach the good news of God's acceptance all across the countryside and to possess nothing as he did so. In doing this, he tried to step back across 1200 years of history to emulate Jesus and the earliest disciples. Like them, Francis resolved to own nothing so that nothing owned him.

That spring, bracing against heavy ridicule, Francis stood in the piazzas of Assisi and other nearby towns preaching the gospel of God's forgiveness in Jesus Christ and the practice of poverty. Francis was revolted by the materialism and unscrupulous pursuit of wealth that he saw all around him. He was convinced that materialism had seriously undermined the morals of his age. Francis was shocked by the wealth and splendor of some of the clergy. It seemed utterly inconsistent to him that servants of the poor Galilean should live as though they were rich. He denounced money itself as being a demon and a curse and bade his hearers to despise money as if it were dung. He called on men and women to sell all that they had and give the proceeds to the poor.

Small audiences listened to Francis' preaching with wonder and with growing admiration. But most people simply passed him by, taking him for a fool. Francis lived and worked this way for three years before he made any converts; then he was joined by Bernard of Quintavelle, another rich man from Assisi.

Soon other hearts were moved by Francis' preaching and example. A dozen men offered to follow his doctrine and his way of life. Francis welcomed them and gave them Jesus' words from Matthew 10:7-10 as their commission from Christ and their rule for life. They made themselves brown robes and built cabins out of branches around the chapel of San Damiano.

Rejecting the older form of monasticism, in which the monks sought to live separate lives of holiness and isolation, they ventured forth daily—barefoot and penniless—to preach the gospel of Jesus Christ on the highways and byways. Often they would travel for several days, sleep in haylofts, and beg for food as they visited distant cities, leper colonies, hospitals, orphanages, and anywhere the burden of human need seemed most acute.

Eventually, in 1210, Francis and the twelve brothers went to visit Pope Innocent III; and the Pope recognized the spirituality and simplicity of these men. They were granted permission to preach the gospel everywhere and were commissioned as the *Fratres Minores*—"the Friars Minor." "Friars" means "brothers." They were not "fathers" or priests. "Minor" implies being lowly—the least of Christ's servants, commissioned to work among the lowly and the outcasts. As Bonaventure wrote,

> Holy poverty,
> which was all they had to meet their expenses,
> made them prompt for obedience,
> robust for work and free for travel.
> Because they possessed nothing that belonged to the world,
> they were attached to nothing and feared to lose nothing.
> They were safe everywhere,
> not held back by fear, nor distracted by care;
> they lived with untroubled minds,
> and, without any anxiety,
> looked forward to the morrow
> and to finding a lodging for the night.
> In different parts of the world
> many insults were hurled against them
> as persons unknown and despised.
> But their love for the Gospel of Christ
> had made them so patient
> that they sought
> to be where they would suffer physical persecution
> rather than where their holiness was recognized
> and they could glory in worldly honor.

> Their very poverty
> seemed to them overflowing abundance
> since, according to the advice of the wise man,
> they were content *with a minimum*
> *as if it were much.*[6]

One of the people deeply affected by Francis' preaching and example was Clare di Favarone. She was the third child of another wealthy family of Assisi. Clare was a devout Christian even before she heard Francis preach in 1210; but on hearing him, she embraced a Franciscan approach to Christian life. Her family opposed this development and sought instead to have her married into another prominent family. Clare, however, entered the Benedictine monastery of San Paolo in 1212. At one of the first chapels Francis restored, Clare subsequently established a community for women based on the principles Francis taught. As like-minded women joined her in that work, the "Poor Ladies of Assisi," or "Poor Clares," were formed. Clare maintained a powerful preaching and teaching ministry, principally among women, and wrote many letters of spiritual counsel (some of which have survived). In a letter she wrote to Anges of Prague, Clare extolled the virtues of God-centered poverty:

> O blessed poverty,
>> who bestows eternal riches on those who love and
>> embrace her!
> O holy poverty,
>> to those who possess and desire you
>> God promises *the kingdom of heaven*
>> and offers, indeed, eternal glory and blessed life!
> O God-centered poverty,
>> whom the Lord Jesus Christ
>> Who ruled and now rules heaven and earth,
>> *Who spoke and things were* made [Ps. 32:9, 148:5]
>> condescended to embrace before all else![7]

Poverty is such a horrible problem in many parts of our world that it is difficult to understand Francis and Clare's advocacy for poverty. Their testimony, however, was not merely an advocacy for poverty. Poverty was not thrust on them by the circumstances of their lives. They chose poverty in order to stand in solidarity with the poor and in order to become their helpers and advocates. Francis and Clare chose to renounce possessions and wealth because of the way those things tend to turn our attention away from a wholehearted focus on God. Hence, their advocacy for poverty was, at its foundation, an advocacy for putting God first in a person's life—putting God ahead of material things and possessions. It was a determined effort to stand in solidarity with the poor as their friend and helper.

Prayer

Holy God, help me not to seek security, identity, or status through the things of this world. I know that I am more than what I have or can ever have. Help me rather to find my security and my identity in you and in my Lord, Jesus Christ. Grant that some of the spirit of Francis and Clare might grow in me so that I might be willing to have less so that others (who have nothing) may have more. Help me find ways I can express Jesus' compassion for the poor. Like Francis and Clare, help me live more simply so that others may simply live. Let this be so. In Jesus' name I pray. **Amen.**

Questions for Reflection

1. How do you think Francis and Clare would respond to contemporary Christianity as you experience it?

2. What do you think of Francis' determination to own nothing so that nothing would own him? How did this sharpen his focus on living for Jesus Christ?

3. Does the desire to live a less materialistic, less economically focused life seem consistent with the teachings and example of Jesus Christ? Why or why not?

4. What tangible steps can contemporary Christians take to live a less materialistic, more Christ-centered life?

5. What lifestyle changes can you and your family make that would help you live a simpler and more God-focused life?

For Further Reading

Francis and Clare: The Complete Works, translated by Regis Armstrong and Ignatius C. Brady (Paulist Press, 1982).

Saint Francis of Assisi, by G.K. Chesterton (Doubleday Image Books, 1957).

Bonaventure: The Soul's Journey Into God, The Tree of Life, and The Life of St. Francis, translated by Ewert Cousins (Paulist Press, 1978).

The Little Flowers of St. Francis of Assisi, translated by H. Heywood (Vantage Press, 1998).

Notes

[1] From "The Life of St. Francis," in *Bonaventure: The Soul's Journey Into God, The Tree of Life, and The Life of St. Francis*, translated by Ewert Cousins (Paulist Press, 1978).

[2] From *Bonaventure: The Soul's Journey Into God, The Tree of Life, and The Life of St. Francis*; page 191.

[3] From *Bonaventure: The Soul's Journey Into God, The Tree of Life, and The Life of St. Francis*; page 192.

[4] From *Francis and Clare: The Complete Works*, translated by Regis J. Armstrong and Ignatius C. Brady (Paulist Press, 1982); page 103.

[5] From *Bonaventure: The Soul's Journey Into God, The Tree of Life, and The Life of St. Francis*; page 199.

[6] From *Bonaventure: The Soul's Journey Into God, The Tree of Life, and The Life of St. Francis*; pages 211–212.

[7] From *Francis and Clare: The Complete Works*; page 192.

VI

Thomas Aquinas
(1225–1274)

Faith and Reason

Christianity has had a rather ambiguous attitude toward the relationship of faith and reason. To some degree this ambivalence reaches back to Scripture itself. We are told, for example, "Now faith is the assurance of things hoped for, the conviction of things not seen" (Hebrews 11:1). Yet we are also urged, "Be ready to make your defense to anyone who demands from you an accounting for the hope that is in you" (1 Peter 3:15). These texts remind us that our faith has rational reasons associated with it, and yet many of the most-profound aspects of faith remain unseen. Contemporary Christians sometimes find themselves troubled by the stark contrasts that are drawn between the world of science or medicine and the world of faith—between the seen and the unseen. Sometimes it is difficult to find the point of connection between our hearts and our minds, between our faith and the physical world around us.

* * * *

Thomas Aquinas was the seventh and last son of Count Landulf of Aquino. His father was a member of the Italian nobility, and his mother descended from French nobility. A distant relative of the Holy Roman Emperor, Thomas was born in the castle at Rocca Secca, near Naples, Italy. Great things were expected of him. While his family hoped he would embark on a career that made the most of his station in life, Thomas seemed from the earliest of ages to be drawn toward a religious life. One incident, often described by his biographers, will stand for many others: "One day, as his nurse was going to bathe him, little Tommaso grasped a piece of parchment which no amount of pleading would convince him to give up. He wept so copiously that it was necessary to bathe him with his hand closed. His mother came, and despite his crying and screaming, opened the hand by force; on the piece of parchment the [prayer] 'Hail Mary' was written."[1]

A stout and silent child, Thomas was subsequently called "the Dumb Ox" by his fellow students at the University of Cologne, not because of his intellectual abilities (which were extraordinary), but due to his solemn and quiet demeanor. Even as a child Thomas seemed to be lost in his own thoughts, only to break out of them occasionally with a startling question. "What is God?" the five-year-old Tommaso asked when he entered the abbey school at nearby Monte Cassino. There he learned to love the spirituality and devotional practices associated with the Benedictine Order that operated the abbey.

When Thomas was fifteen or sixteen years of age, the political intrigue that shaped both Church and state forced his father to withdraw him from the abbey school. Thomas was sent to the University of Naples to further his education. He excelled in his studies there, showing a brilliance that would characterize his long academic career. The Dominican Order, which was an order of preachers and teachers, had established a school of theology that was affiliated with the University of Naples. Despite his great love for the Benedictine tradition, during this time Thomas felt a strong call on his heart urging him to begin a religious life in the Dominican Order.

Thomas' parents were opposed to his desire to join the Dominicans. His parents thought that traveling from place to place without food, extra clothing, or a place to stay would be too extreme a life for their son. They had earlier reconciled themselves to his desire to embark on the religious life and hoped that one day he would be installed as abbot at the nearby abbey of Monte Cassino. That would be a suitable position for a person of Thomas' heritage, rank, and station; and it would be a position from which he could enhance the power and authority of his family.

The prospect of a cloistered life at Monte Cassino did not appeal to Thomas, however. Whether it was the apostolic poverty of the mendicant Dominicans (a "begging order") or their commitment to teaching and preaching the Word of God that appealed to him, Thomas left Naples resolved to join the Dominicans. But his brothers hatched a plan to circumvent Thomas' resolve. They kidnapped Thomas and held him captive in his own room at Castle Rocca Secca for more than a year.

Thomas' response to this intervention was to turn his room into a place of monastic retreat. He retained the habit and spiritual disciplines of his order, studied the Bible, and read the standard theological works of the day. His brothers responded by sneaking a "pretty young girl, with all the charms of a temptress"[2] into his room—hoping that their brother would succumb to the temptations of the flesh and disqualify himself for the religious life he sought. Thomas responded by leaping from his bed, snatching a firebrand from the glowing embers on the hearth, and chasing the prostitute from the room. Undeterred, he continued his monastic seclusion and used it as an opportunity to instruct his sisters.

Thomas' eldest sister, Marotta, became a devoted disciple of the Benedictine tradition through his influence. His mother, too, seemed to fall under his spiritual influence; and she eventually helped him slip past the surveillance of his brothers. He climbed out of a window and made his way to Naples. From Naples he went on to the convent of Saint-Jacques, in Paris, where he served three years as a novice in the Dominican Order. At Saint-Jacques, Thomas met a man whose influence would shape the rest of his life, Albertus Magnus (1193–1280).

Albertus was the most-famous Christian intellectual of the twelfth century. He was called "Magnus"—which is Latin for "the Great"—even by other well-respected philosophers and theologians. The breadth and depth of his knowledge was unsurpassed. It encompassed many fertile fields, including astronomy, chemistry, philosophy, physics, theology, and music. His collected writings spanned thirty-eight volumes, and there seemed to be no important matter that Albertus Magnus left unexplored. For this reason he was called "the Universal Doctor."

The bedrock assumption on which all of Magnus' work stood was his belief that truth—wherever it was found—ultimately leads directly to a knowledge of God. Or, in the words of a contemporary cliché, "All truth is God's truth." This faith assumption gave him both the freedom and the responsibility to pursue truth wherever he found it as part of his religious vocation. It also gave him an utter passion to demonstrate the unity of all truth under God.

Albertus intended to integrate all knowledge into a pattern shaped by his Christian faith and in so doing develop a Christian worldview. Albertus passed on his passion for the unity of truth to his most-able disciple, Thomas Aquinas. This passion along with his childhood question, "What is God?" would shape Thomas' life and career for the next three decades. Soon he would follow Albertus Magnus to the University of Cologne, in Germany, where he studied for four years. At the end of that time, Master Albert recommended Thomas for a teaching position at the convent of Saint-Jacques; and Thomas embarked on his professorial career. During this period the first of many, many books and treatises began streaming from his productive pen.

Beginning in 1259, Thomas spent nine years in Italy, generally working at the request of the Church on various projects in diverse locations. Thomas' knowledge and productivity were so expansive that he no longer wrote with his own hand but dictated his writings to three or four secretaries who wrote down his thoughts on as many different subjects. This intellectual brilliance was an ironic contrast to Aquinas' physical appearance and his silent, distracted demeanor. Thomas' biographer Chesterton remarked, "His bulk made it easy to regard him humorously as [a] sort of walking wine-barrel."[3] His silent demeanor and the stark contrast between his intellect and his physical form earned Thomas the nickname "the Dumb Ox." Chesterton wryly suggested that it was Thomas himself who joked about his size: "It may be that he...was responsible for the sublime exaggeration that a crescent was cut out of the dinner table to allow him to sit down. It is quite certain that it was an exaggeration; and that his stature was more remarked than his stoutness; but, above all, that his head was quite powerful enough to dominate his body."[4]

Thomas Aquinas' eyes were what seemed to capture everyone's attention, however. "There is kindled in them," Chesterton wrote, "a fire of instant inner excitement; they are vivid and very Italian eyes. The man is thinking about something; and something that has reached a crisis; not about nothing or about anything; or what is almost worse, about everything. There must have been that smouldering vigilance in his eyes."[5]

Thomas' early lectures in Paris took formal shape when he returned to Italy; and they provided the basis for one of his most-famous works: *Summa Contra Gentiles*, which is Latin for "Summary Against the Gentiles." Written between 1261 and 1264, at the request of Saint Raymond of Peñafort, it was a great defense of the Christian faith. *Summa Contra Gen-*

tiles was addressed to scholarly Muslims who had captured most of Spain and established a colony there. Aquinas shared with these Moors a profound respect for the philosophy of Aristotle. Indeed, his quest to produce a unity of all knowledge (including philosophy and theology) caused Thomas to "baptize" Aristotle's ideas and use them as a support and defense for the Christian faith. Thus in *Summa Contra Gentiles*, Aquinas intended to use Aristotle's philosophy as an intellectual bridge across which he could deliver Christian truth to non-Christian readers. This same project caused Aquinas to be profoundly interested in the relationship between Christian faith and reason; indeed, he intended to use philosophical reason to under gird and prove the verities of the Christian faith.

Thomas considered the life of the mind to be one of the greatest gifts and greatest undertakings to which people could apply themselves. In *Summa Contra Gentiles* he wrote,

> Of all human pursuits, the pursuit of wisdom is the more perfect, the more sublime, the more useful, and the more agreeable. The more perfect, because in so far as a man gives himself up to the pursuit of wisdom, to that extent he enjoys already some portion of true happiness. *Blessed is the man that shall dwell in wisdom* (Ecclus. xiv, 22). The more sublime, because thereby man comes closest to the likeness of God, who *hath made all things in wisdom* (Ps. ciii, 24). The more useful, because by this same wisdom we arrive at the realm of immortality. *The desire of wisdom shall lead to an everlasting kingdom* (Wisd. vi, 21). The more agreeable, because *her conversation hath no bitterness, nor her company any weariness, but gladness and joy* (Wisd. viii, 16).[6]

This pursuit of godly wisdom, Thomas believed, was possible and necessary because he could use it to confute the errors of "the Gentiles" and lead the "Mohammedans and Pagans" to faith even though they did not accept the authority of the Christian Scriptures.[7]

Thomas began his work with a prayer and continued it in a profound attitude of prayer. He wrote (in part),

> Thou Who makest eloquent the tongues of little children, fashion my words and pour on my lips the grace of Thy benediction. Grant me penetration to understand, capacity to retain, method and faculty in study, subtlety in interpretation and abundant grace of expression.
>
> Order the beginning, direct the progress and perfect the achievement of my work, Thou Who art true God and true Man and livest and reignest for ever and ever. Amen."[8]

From Scripture and from Aristotle, Aquinas learned that the truth about God could be demonstrated through "natural reason" by pointing to examples in creation and the natural world. In this way Thomas embraced Aristotle's belief that ideas come into the human mind through the five senses (hearing, sight, sound, taste, and touch); this was an early form of empiricism, or the scientific method. As Thomas himself wrote, "Everything that is in the intellect has been in the senses."[9] This was a complete break with Anselm and earlier Christian thinkers, who believed that ideas came from within the human mind as a kind of reflection of the divine mind. Aquinas' approach to the question of knowing led to the belief that we come to know things by looking at the physical world around us. This was the fundamental assumption on which modern culture and science would be built.

In this way, then, Aquinas used Aristotle's proof for the existence of God, based on the consideration of motion in the world, as a basis for talking to non-Christians about the Christian God. "Everything that is in motion," he wrote, "is put and kept in motion by some other thing. It is evident to sense that there are beings in motion. A thing is in motion because something else puts and keeps it in motion. That mover therefore either is itself in motion or not. If it is not in motion, our point is gained which we propose to prove, namely, that we must posit something which moves other things without being itself in motion, and this we call God."[10] Hence, God is viewed as the "Unmoved Mover" who sets the universe in motion.

In a similar way, Aristotle's argument for the existence of God, based on the notion of there being a "first cause," lent itself to Thomas' apologetic approach: "The Philosopher also goes about in another way to show that it is impossible to proceed to infinity in the series of efficient causes, but we must come to one first cause, and this we call God."[11]

Summa Contra Gentiles established Thomas' theological method solidly in his own mind. "The Philosopher" (Aristotle) would be followed as a bridge to the Truth, so far as the bridge would take him; then the truths of Scripture and Christian tradition would be added to those of philosophy in order to explain the Christian faith and prove its cogency. This was also the approach Aquinas followed in his greatest and most far-reaching work, *Summa Theologica* ("Summary of Theology"). He intended the work to be a well-reasoned introduction to the Christian faith, but Thomas' love for detail and his compulsion for completeness soon turned it into the first theological encyclopedia.

Penned between 1265 and 1274 while he was working in Paris and then in Naples, the massive *Summa Theologica* would be the most-complete work written by one person, even down into the twentieth century. In it Aquinas elaborated his famous "Five Ways" for proving the existence of God (which he had begun in *Summa Contra Gentiles*). In addition to the First Mover and Efficient Cause (described above), Thomas added arguments based on Contingency (God created the world out of nothing, and everything depends on this event for its existence.), Goodness (There is a gradation of goodness found among created things; this scale of goodness stems from God who is the Highest Good.), and Design (We observe in the world patterns of governance and connection, a pattern of design; this design presupposes a Divine Designer.).

In this way Thomas Aquinas harnessed reason to the wagon of faith and used it to take the explanation and proof of Christian faith as far as it would go. Thomas was not a sheer rationalist, however; he did not believe that reason could create faith. He believed that faith was also rooted in religious experience and mystery. In fact, one day in 1273, Aquinas stopped working on his *Summa Theologica*. Returning to his room after having a profound sense of the presence of Jesus Christ in the Lord's Supper, he said, "I can write no more." [12] After a period of awkward silence, one of his friends inquired further, to which Thomas replied, "I can write no more. I have seen things which make all my writings like straw."[13] This from "the Dumb Ox" who was one of the greatest intellects the world has ever known.

Aquinas teaches us that the same God who made the physical world also made the human mind; that there is a deep and satisfying relationship between human thought and religious faith, between the seen and the unseen, between the head and the heart. Because all truth is God's truth, the life of the mind and the life of the heart can live harmoniously together. Aquinas reminds us that faith in the unseen God is not merely a leap into irrationality. For Aquinas, and perhaps for us, faith in God is a reasonable assent to a chain of physical evidence that we can see in the world (Causation, Movement, Design, Order, Goodness), which urges us to look beyond the physical world for its ultimate Source. We can have a sense of "assurance" because of things that we can see and observe, and this leads us toward "the conviction of things not seen" (Hebrews 11:1). Christian faith confirms the truths that are available to us through rational inquiry, just as our hearts feel and experience the truth that we know and affirm in our minds.

Prayer

Loving God, you are the source of all wisdom! Thank you for giving me both a heart and a mind, for giving me tools and encouragement for growing my faith as well as tools and opportunities for growing my reason and knowledge. Grant that I might use both my faith and my reason to serve you! Teach me not only to grow in Christian faith but also to mature in Christian wisdom. Help me to believe profoundly, and help me to think Christianly. Grant that these resources that far too often have been separated may form for me one path of adoration and service that leads directly to you. Help me serve you with all of my intellect and all of my heart. In Jesus' name I pray. **Amen.**

Questions for Reflection

1. How do you think of the relationship between faith and reason? How do they work together? How are they different?

2. Thomas Aquinas' approach applies reason to the things of the natural world and faith to the things of religious experience and Christian teaching. Does this help you sort out the respective roles of faith and reason? If so, how?

3. Is it possible to have true faith without having reasons for it?

4. Is it possible to prove all aspects of the Christian faith? What aspects of our faith transcend reason or proof?

5. How can you develop reasons for your faith? How can you cultivate a sense of mystery to invigorate your faith?

For Further Reading

Saint Thomas Aquinas: The Dumb Ox, by G.K. Chesterton (Image Books/Doubleday, 1956).

Aquinas, by F.C. Copleston (Penguin Books, 1955).

Notes

[1] From *St. Thomas Aquinas,* by Jacques Maritain. This fine biography of Aquinas can be read at http:/maritain.nd.edu/jmc/etext/thomas1.htm.

[2] From *St. Thomas Aquinas,* by Jacques Maritain; see http:/maritain.nd.edu/jmc/etext/thomas1.htm.

[3] From *Saint Thomas Aquinas,* by G.K. Chesterton (Image Books/Doubleday, 1956); page 97.

[4] From *Saint Thomas Aquinas,* by G.K. Chesterton; page 121.

[5] From *Saint Thomas Aquinas,* by G.K. Chesterton; page 99.

[6] From "Of God and His Creatures," in *Summa Contra Gentiles,* by Thomas Aquinas; 1.2. The text is located at http://www2.nd.edu/Departments/Maritain/etext/gcl_2.htm.

[7] From "Of God and His Creatures," in *Summa Contra Gentiles,* by Thomas Aquinas; 1.2. The text is located at http://www2.nd.edu/Departments/Maritain/etext/gcl_2.htm.

[8] From *St. Thomas Aquinas,* by Jacques Maritain; see http:/maritain.nd.edu/jmc/etext/thomas1.htm.

[9] From *Saint Thomas Aquinas,* by G.K. Chesterton; page 134.

[10] From "Of God and His Creatures," in *Summa Contra Gentiles,* by Thomas Aquinas; 1.13. The text is located at http:/maritain.nd.edu/jmc/etext/thomas1.htm.

[11] From "Of God and His Creatures," in *Summa Contra Gentiles,* by Thomas Aquinas; 1.13. The text is located at http:/maritain.nd.edu/jmc/etext/thomas1.htm.

[12] From *Saint Thomas Aquinas,* by G.K. Chesterton; page 116.

[13] From *Saint Thomas Aquinas,* by G.K. Chesterton; page 116.

VII

Catherine of Siena
(1347–1380)

The Way of Perfection

We sometimes feel that the challenges and problems surrounding us are too large for our puny faith to handle. We think we are too ordinary and too insignificant for our witness to make much impact on the great scheme of things. Perhaps life has dealt us what looks like a bad "hand," and it feels like we are disqualified from really living or from rising above the challenges we face. Catherine of Siena was a "nobody" from whom no one expected much of anything. Yet she had a great love for Christ and a passion for Christian service, and ultimately these things made a tremendous difference in her and in her world.

* * * *

Catherine Benincasa was born in 1347 in Siena, Italy. She was the twenty-third child of the twenty-five born to a prosperous cloth dyer named Giacomo Benincasa. The times in which she lived were extremely tumultuous ones for the Church and for society. Pope Boniface VIII had been pressing the papacy's territorial and temporal claims to the point that he enraged Philip IV, the king of France. In a power struggle over dominance in northern Italy, the French king was victorious over the Italian pope insofar as he was able to get a French pontiff (Clement V) elected after Boniface's death in 1303. Under the French pope the papacy relocated to Avignon, France, where it hoped to thrive under the protection and influence of the French monarchy. For Christians living outside of France, however, this period was known as "the Babylonian Captivity" of the papacy, since it symbolized (like the biblical precedent) that the Pope was living in a foreign land, under foreign control.

The bubonic plague, which was called the "Black Death," swept through Siena and the other Italian cities beginning in 1349, claiming the lives of one-third of the population. Since its causes were unknown to even the intellectual elite, superstition mingled with ignorance; and people attributed the plague to God's judgment, witches, or a demonic curse on society. Amidst these somber situations, the Italian city-states were also quarreling among themselves in bouts of sibling rivalry that played out in armed struggles for economic and political dominance.

Catherine's life—even her early life—stood out as a stark contrast against this background of death, depression, and turmoil. Catherine was a happy child, so joyful that her father gave her the nickname "Euphrosyne," which is Greek for "Joy." [1] It was also the name of a Christian saint from the fifth century who turned her back on marriage so that she could give herself completely to Jesus Christ in a kind of spiritual marriage.

At the tender age of seven, Catherine had a dramatic religious experience in which she had a vision of the risen Christ seated in glory with Peter, Paul, and John. In the aftermath of this vision, she made a secret vow to give her whole self and her whole life to God. Spiritually precocious from this point onward, Catherine seemed drawn to a life of prayer and solitude. Prayer became for her a source of tremendous joy and happiness.

A vivacious and attractive girl, Catherine's parents hoped that she would have a happy marriage that would be a credit to her family. When Catherine turned twelve, her mother began to urge her to dress in the fancy gowns and wear the makeup and jewelry that polite society required of women of her age. Catherine complied with these expectations, in large part to please her parents; but she was soon smitten in her conscience about engaging in so much frivolity. She told her parents that she had decided that she would never marry. They responded by pressing the issue with her, even going so far as trying to find her a husband.

Catherine reacted by chopping off her long honey-brown hair, which her parents said was her greatest mark of beauty. She, however, saw it as her greatest vanity. Catherine's parents responded to her rebellion by forcing her to live a sort of "Cinderella" life—doing the dishes, cleaning, and performing other household chores that were usually assigned to servants. Perhaps more challenging from Catherine's point of view was their resolve to take from her those periods of prayerful solitude that she craved and that had become the source of her spiritual joy. Catherine reacted by finding a deeper, inner peace that remained untouched by outward turmoil. She bore these punishments with such patience and love that her parents soon relented and repented of their attempts to dissuade Catherine from following a radical path of Christian spirituality.

When Catherine's parents relented and allowed her to follow her own desires, she established a monastic cell in their home. There she lived a life of prayer, reflection, and solitude. She practiced many forms of self-denial, sleeping on a hard board and wearing a rough shirt under her outer clothing. She slept and ate little, dedicating herself instead to prayer and fasting. Sometimes she imposed long periods of seclusion or silence on herself. In short, in following her radical Christian desires along the lines established by her spiritual context and times, Catherine became an ascetic who practiced disciplines of self-denial. She practiced these disciplines in order to become devoid of self-will and selfishness and to become more completely conformed to the will of Jesus Christ. During this period of seclusion Catherine began to have visions and other mystical experiences that drew her closer and closer to Christ.

Uneducated and unable to read and write, as were most women of her day, Catherine was permitted to join the Dominican Order as a lay-sister (tertiary) who committed her life to Christ through prayer and Christian service. From then on she wore the white habit and black mantle of the Dominicans. Even though she was allowed to continue to live in her own home, she followed the rules and spiritual disciplines of her order. Soon a spiritual "family" began to gather around Catherine as women and men came to appreciate her spirituality and visited her seeking religious advice. Among these followers would be several priests who became Catherine's disciples and confessors. They also put her teachings into writing and took letters at her dictation.

Catherine's point of view was extremely attractive, over against the trials of her times, because she stressed a holy joy that was operative in a person's life through God's love. Her Christian joy stood in utter contrast to the somber tenor of her times. Her emphasis on personal holiness was like a breath of fresh air in a church that was far too taken up with wealth, politics, and corruption.

Catherine's brand of spirituality would, subsequently, become enshrined in *The Dialogue* (1378). This remarkable book is a conversation between the faithful soul and God in which God tells the soul how to live a Christ-like life.

In describing "The Way of Perfection," Catherine said that the Christian must have "infinite desire" and not infinite, self-imposed suffering; "for God," she dictated, "who is infinite, would have [from us] infinite love and infinite sorrow."[2] Echoing Jesus' "greatest commandment" (Matthew 22:36-38), Catherine taught that this "infinite sorrow" is to be twofold; it is a sorrow for our offenses against God our Creator and for our offenses against our neighbors. The "infinite love" of Catherine's directive amounts to, "You shall love the Lord your God with all your heart, and with all your soul, and with all your mind.... You shall love your neighbor as yourself" (Matthew 22:37-38). As Catherine also pointed out, this is the "infinite love" of 1 Corinthians 13: "So the glorious apostle Paul taught: 'If I had an angelic tongue, knew the future, gave what is mine to the poor, and gave my body to be burned, but did not have charity, it would be worth nothing to me.' Finite works are not enough either to punish or to atone unless they are seasoned with loving charity."[3]

Catherine's path to this sort of holy love was a Christ-centered way that looked to the Lord as the source of our love and holiness. Receiving and cultivating Christ's love within leads to holiness, and holiness produces true humility. Hence, Catherine heard God tell her, in her inmost soul,

> No virtue can have life in it except from charity [the Latin (*charitas*) means "sacrificial love"], and charity is nursed and mothered by humility. You will find humility in the knowledge of yourself when you see that even your own experience comes not from yourself but from me, for I loved you before you came into being. And in my unspeakable love for you I willed to create you anew in grace. So I washed you and made you a new creation in the blood that my only-begotten Son poured out with such burning love.[4]

Catherine believed that every personal vice and every Christian virtue will be put into action through a person's relationship with his or her neighbors. The Lord told her, "I would have you know that every virtue and every vice is put into action by means of your neighbors. If you hate me, you harm your neighbors, and yourself as well (for you are your chief neighbor), and the harm is both general and particular."[5] This "charity" or selfless Christian love that Catherine advocated is not simply an ideal;

it is to be lived out in the context of real life relationships ("your neighbor and yourself"). Hence, God told her,

> It is your duty to love your neighbors as your own self [Lev. 19:18; Mk. 12:33]. In love you ought to help them spiritually with prayer and counsel, and assist them spiritually and materially in their need—at least with your good will if you have nothing else. If you do not love me you do not love your neighbors, nor will you help those you do not love. But it is yourself you harm most, because you deprive yourself of grace. And you harm your neighbors by depriving them of the prayer and loving desires you should be offering to me on their behalf. Every help you give them ought to come from the affection you bear them for the love of me.[6]

As the plague ravaged Siena in 1374, Catherine and her spiritual "family" worked tirelessly with the stricken, even though two of her own brothers and one sister died in the onslaught. As Catherine's earliest biography reported, "The charity infused into the heart of this holy maiden was such that . . . she [was] almost continuously aiding her neighbors by works of charity."[7]

Catherine of Siena was not only a spiritual leader, a mystic, and a social activist, she was also an ecclesiastical reformer. She was greatly pained about the state of the Church in her day; and in 1375 she began to write (through the priests who had become her disciples and confessors and who wrote letters at her dictation) to the French pope, Gregory XI, who was ensconced in Avignon, France. Her letters were all written "In the Name of Jesus Christ crucified and of sweet Mary." Combining a deep reverence and a spiritual familiarity, which was startling for her rank and times, Catherine consistently addressed the pontiff as "Sweetest Daddy." After showing appropriate love and concern for Gregory XI and the Church, Catherine indicated that she was concerned that the Pope had not adequately separated himself from worldly concerns and the desire to please his contemporaries. She felt that this was a serious failing in a Christian leader.

> I say, then: if he is a prelate, he does ill, because to avoid falling into disfavour with his fellow-creatures—that is, through self-love—in which he is bound by self-indulgence—holy justice dies in him. For he sees his subjects commit faults and sins, and pretends not to see them and fails to correct them; or if he does correct them, he does it with such coldness and lukewarmness that he does not accomplish anything, but plasters vice over; and he is always afraid of giving displeasure or of getting into a quarrel.[8]

This, in her view, described what was going wrong in Gregory's pontificate (1370–1378); and she urged him to correct it: "I hope by the goodness of God venerable father mine, that you will quench this [self love] in yourself, and will not love yourself for yourself, nor your neighbour for yourself, nor God."[9]

In addition to this kind of spiritual insight, which had direct bearing on the conduct of the Church, Catherine also was willing to give Pope Gregory advice about very practical matters, such as appointing cardinals. Too often he had appointed cardinals for political reasons; so in a letter she said, "I have heard here that you have appointed the cardinals. I believe that it would honour God and profit us more if you would take heed always to appoint virtuous men. If the contrary is done, it will be a great insult to God, and disaster to Holy Church. Let us not wonder later if God sends us His disciplines and scourges; for the thing is just. I beg you to do what you have to do manfully and in the fear of God."[10]

A second letter from Catherine was soon forthcoming:

Most holy and most reverend my father in Christ Jesus: I Catherine your poor unworthy daughter, servant and slave of the servants of Christ, write to you in His precious Blood; with desire to see you a good shepherd. For I reflect, sweet my "Babbo" [Tuscan: "daddy"], that the wolf is carrying away your sheep, and there is no one found to help them. So I hasten to you, our father and our shepherd, begging you on behalf of Christ crucified to learn from Him, who with such fire of love gave Himself to the shameful death of the most holy Cross, to rescue that lost sheep, the human race.[11]

Catherine returned to her love theology in this second letter, graphically describing the love with which Christ has loved all humans: "So then with love He has drawn us, and has conquered our malice with His benignness, in so much that every heart should be drawn to Him: since greater love one cannot show—and this He Himself said—than to give one's life for one's friend....What, then, shall we say of that most burning and complete love which gave its life for its foes?"[12]

Catherine urged Gregory to be full of the "burning and complete" love of Christ as he led the Church. She urged him to use this love to win back the "lost sheep": "Holiest sweet 'Babbo' mine, I see no other way for us, and no other help in winning back your sheep, which have left the fold of Holy Church in rebellion, not obedient nor subject to you, their father. I pray you therefore, on behalf of Christ crucified, and I will that you do me this grace, to overcome their malice with your benignity."[13]

The nobles of Florence were having a political and economic quarrel with Pope Gregory XI. He responded by putting them under papal interdict, which censured them by denying them (among other things) the comforts of the sacraments and Christian burial. In 1376, the nobles of Florence begged Catherine of Siena to intercede with them at the papal court. She agreed to go, but her errand was her own; she accepted the mission as an opportunity to try to convince the French pope to move the Papal See back to Rome. While the exact words she spoke to him have been lost to posterity, Catherine's faith and witness were extremely persuasive; and Gregory XI did return to Rome, where he died in 1378.

Worn out by the rigors of her spiritual disciplines and her many ministries, Catherine dictated her spiritual classic *Dialogue of the Soul* and soon followed Gregory in death in 1380. She was only thirty-three years old.

Catherine of Siena, the diminutive daughter of a cloth dyer, is remembered as a spiritual giant who was mighty in prayer and full of the love of Christ. She was a nurse to the sick, a friend of the poor, and a holy reformer of the Church at a time when such ministries were in short supply. Her example reminds us that even very ordinary people can rise to extraordinary heights of usefulness and service when they give themselves wholeheartedly to God in faith. Catherine's commitment to Christ and Christian service transformed her life by an infusion of the power of God's love. Under such circumstances, one person can make an extraordinary difference in the lives of friends; family; and, indeed, the world.

Prayer

Lord Jesus Christ, sometimes I feel so small and insignificant that I wonder in frustration, "What difference can one person make?" Grant, Lord, that the next time I feel this way you will bring Catherine of Siena to my mind. Help me to know that you have made me for yourself—a very special person full of good gifts and talents that I am even now discovering. Like Catherine, help me to live my life as a vessel of your love. Like her, help me turn to you again and again to be renewed, transformed, and filled by your love. Fill me so full of your love that my fears and inadequacies are extinguished. In your powerful name I pray. **Amen.**

Questions for Reflection

1. Catherine of Siena found in "the greatest commandment" (Matthew 22:36-38) a transforming life principle. How does the single-minded love for God empower us to serve our neighbor? How does this same agape (self-giving) love help us see ourselves in a new and different light?

2. Catherine's radical commitment to Christ allowed her, a very ordinary person, to have an extraordinary impact on the lives of others and on the Church of her day. How can a greater focus on the love of Christ in your life also have an impact on those around you? On your family? your friends? your church?

3. Among Catherine's remarkable virtues were a deep-seated joy in Christ and a profound humility. How can Christian love make you a more joy-filled person? How can Christian love become an avenue to deep and genuine humility?

4. Catherine had the courage (borrowing the Quaker phrase) "to speak truth to power," and she was remarkably successful in influencing Pope Gregory XI in positive ways. Why do you think she was so successful with Gregory XI? What might we learn from her example?

Suggestions for Further Reading

Catherine of Siena: The Dialogue, edited and translated by Suzanne Noffke (Paulist Press, 1980).

The Life of St. Catherine of Siena, by Raymond of Capua (Tan Books and Publishers, 2003).

St. Catherine of Siena as Seen in Her Letters, translated by Vida Scudder (J.M. Dent, 1905). Reprinted by Kessinger Press, 2004. The full text of this work is also available at "Project Gutenberg," at http://www.gutenberg.org/dirs/exte05/7ltcb10.txt.

Notes

[1] From *The Life of St. Catherine of Siena*, by Raymond of Capua (Tan Books and Publishers, 2003); page 23.

[2] From *Catherine of Siena: The Dialogue*, translated by Suzanne Noffke (Paulist Press, 1980); page 28.

[3] From *Catherine of Siena: The Dialogue*; page 29.

[4] From *Catherine of Siena: The Dialogue*; page 29.

[5] From *Catherine of Siena: The Dialogue*; page 33.

[6] From *Catherine of Siena: The Dialogue*; pages 33–34.

[7] From *The Life of St. Catherine of Siena*, by Raymond of Capua (Tan Books and Publishers, 2003); page 126.

[8] From *Saint Catherine of Siena as Seen in Her Letters*, translated by Vida D. Scudder (J.M. Dent, 1905); pages 78–79. Reprinted by Kessinger Press, 2004.

[9] From *Saint Catherine of Siena as Seen in Her Letters*; page 79.

[10] From *Saint Catherine of Siena as Seen in Her Letters*; page 81.

[11] From *Saint Catherine of Siena as Seen in Her Letters*; page 83.

[12] From *Saint Catherine of Siena as Seen in Her Letters*; page 84.

[13] From *Saint Catherine of Siena as Seen in Her Letters*; page 84.

VIII

Julian of Norwich
(ca. 1342–1423)

Our True Mother

We humans find it difficult to understand and conceptualize God. As Jesus told the woman at the well in Samaria, "God is spirit" (John 4:24). God is invisible and mysterious, not visible through a telescope or a microscope. But the human mind seems to need some kind of mental picture of God; so following the lead of the Bible, we think of God as a "Father" or as a "Shepherd." These word-pictures are right and accurate for us because they properly remind us that God is like a nurturing Parent or a protecting Guide. In her quest for a deep personal relationship with God, Julian of Norwich found it meaningful to look within her own life experience to find metaphors and word-pictures that described how precious God in Jesus Christ was to her. She communicated the message of God's love in poignant and memorable ways at a time when witnesses of a loving God were desperately needed.

* * * *

In the midst of our harried and hectic lives, we sometimes long for moments of peace, tranquility, prayer, and spiritual reflection. This hunger for holy peace (Hebrew: *shalom*) is precisely what motivated Julian of Norwich to commit herself to the life of a medieval anchoress. Her solitary life in holy seclusion was a life that stands in utter contrast to the life that so many of us live in the modern world.

Julian lived alone in a single room, which was attached to Norwich Cathedral in Norwich, England. Her room had two windows. One window opened into the church, through which she could hear the many services of the cathedral and receive Holy Communion. The other window opened onto the busy world of downtown Norwich. Between these two windows Julian lived a solitary life of prayer, meditation, and sacred enclosure— she had taken vows that precluded her leaving her room. But through a way of life that sounds very strange to us, Julian had found a path to something most medieval women lacked. Paraphrasing the title of Virginia Woolf's well-known essay, she had "a room of her own." She was able to follow her own spiritual compass—one that was shaped by her prayer and by her sense of calling, rather than by the many external forces that so often shape a person's destiny.

The location of her room between Norwich Cathedral and the secular world was a major factor in the success of Julian's ministry. She took the comforts and blessings of prayer and spiritual reflection and offered them to those who stopped under her world-side window. People often came to request intercessory prayer, to raise spiritual questions, and to tell of terrible personal problems. Julian prayed for these people and served as a spiritual director. In these functions she was a mediator between the Church and the world.

The world in which Julian lived was full of crisis and turmoil. King Edward III, who came to power in 1330 by way of the liaison between his adulterous mother and her lover, ruled England with an iron grip. England had been at war against Scotland and France since 1334, in what would be called "The Hundred Years War." It was a long, expensive, and socially debilitating conflict that sapped England of its resources and its people of their zest for life. The Black Death (bubonic plague) ravaged England throughout the century. In 1351, a particularly potent strain, which proved lethal to children, swept across England. Massive crop failures in 1348, 1363, and again in 1369 brought hunger and starvation to (already) war weary, pestilence-ridden people.[1]

The Church, which should have been a source of comfort and strength for her people, too often followed the pattern of the secular world. The papacy was once again divided, this time between Pope Urban VI (who ruled from Rome) and Pope Clement VII (who occupied a rival see in Avignon, France). The Church seemed unable to make sense of the calamities that befell society, and the rival papacies spent most of their time and energy attempting to triumph (spiritually and militarily) over each other. In a similar way, much effort was diverted to hunting down Jews and heretics in superstitious attempts to try to turn aside the plague. Several people had been burned to death within sight of Julian's window on the world.

The sermons offered in the cathedral and those given by the popular preachers who roamed the countryside were full of gloom, doom, and damnation. Many people came to see themselves and their very lives as being lived out under the weight of some kind of divine curse. The main comfort that the Church offered the people came in the form of her sacraments, but these were enshrined in a language many persons did not understand well and were readily becoming a matter of rote performance instead of stimulating pious reflection.[2]

Not much is known about Julian's life. It is assumed because of the accent of her writings that she was from the north of England. She tells us that she was unlettered when she began receiving spiritual revelations from God in her room in 1373. Over the time of her seclusion, she taught herself to read and write so well that her *Revelations of Divine Love* became the first (extant) book written by a woman in the English language.[3] She wrote so movingly of motherhood that even though we do not know this for sure, it is generally assumed that Julian was, as a young woman, both a wife and a mother and that as her children grew and her husband preceded her in death, she felt a strong call to full-time Christian service. Since she had been married, she could not become a nun; but she could become an anchoress (holy solitary) affiliated with the Church.

Beginning in 1373, when she was thirty-and-one-half years of age, Julian (who by this time was living as an anchoress) was visited by a terrible illness. As she lay half dead and paralyzed from the waist down, she received last rites from the Church and prayed for a divine visitation. She asked that in her suffering she might find encouragement in the sufferings of Christ. In response to this prayer she had a vision of Christ crucified. As she described it,

> I saw the red blood trickling down from under the crown [of thorns], all hot, flowing freely and copiously, a living stream, just as it seemed to me that it was at the time when the crown of thorns was thrust down upon his blessed head. Just so did he, both God and man, suffer for me. I perceived, truly and powerfully, that it was himself who showed this to me, without any intermediary; and then I said: "Blessed be the Lord!" This I said with a reverent intention and

a loud voice, and I was greatly astonished by this wonder and marvel, that he would so humbly be with a sinful creature living in this wretched flesh. I accepted it that at that time our Lord Jesus wanted, out of his courteous love, to show me comfort.[4]

Unlike the mediated experiences of Christ, which came to Christians through the sacraments, this was a direct, unmediated experience of Christ and assurance of Christ's love that came directly and personally to Julian. This truth was so etched on her soul that all of her writings and ministry was summarized by her emphasis on the love of Jesus Christ. She wrote, "At the same time as I saw this corporeal sight, our Lord showed me a spiritual sight of his familiar love. I saw that he is to us everything which is good and comforting for our help. He is our clothing, for he is that love which wraps and enfolds us, embraces us and guides us, surrounds us for his love, which is so tender that he may never desert us. And so in this sight I saw truly that he is everything which is good, as I understand."[5]

During this same incident, Julian received a vision or a dream about a hazelnut, which God placed in the palm of her hand. It was so small that it seemed to account for nothing; and as Julian wondered what this could signify, she was given an inner understanding about it. "It lasts and always will, because God loves it; and thus everything has being through the love of God."[6] She was able to derive three spiritual truths from this vision:

The first is that God made it, the second is that he loves it, the third is that God preserves it. But what is that to me? It is that God is the Creator and the lover and the protector. For until I am substantially united to him, I can never have love or rest or true happiness; until, that is, I am so attached to him that there can be no created thing between my God and me. And who will do this deed? Truly, he himself, by his mercy and his grace, for he has made me for this and has blessedly restored me.[7]

Thus, like the writer of the African American spiritual, Julian learned that God "has got the whole world in his hands." More directly, however, God has each person in his hands. Each person matters to God, and each person is an object of God's sacred Son-giving love. Julian derived great strength and encouragement from this insight, and it was also a testimony that she passed on to her readers and to the shattered people who appeared at her window-on-the world to receive spiritual comfort.

Julian received and recorded sixteen visions over the course of her spiritual pilgrimage. These visions provided her with insight and comfort that she passed on to others. Her theology, however, is not experience-centered; it is centered on the Trinity and on the Lord Jesus Christ. One of the interesting developments that stemmed from Julian's experiences with God and from what scholars speculate was her own life experience as a mother was her willingness to think about God as being like a Father and like a Mother to us. At a time when the Church and her preachers tended to think of God as a distant, unapproachable Judge, Julian stressed that God was like a nurturing Parent and a loving Mother. Because of her own fond recollections of family life and her understanding of the parental love of God, Julian was comfortable with using familial metaphors for speaking about God: "And so in our making, God almighty is our loving Father, and God all wisdom is our loving Mother, with the love and goodness of the Holy Spirit, which is all one God, one Lord. And in the joining and the union he is our very true spouse and we his beloved wife and his fair maiden, with which wife he was never displeased; for he says: I love you and you love me, and our love will never divide in two."[8]

The metaphor of God as Mother became particularly poignant to Julian as she began to reflect on her relationship with Jesus Christ. She wrote, for example, "Jesus Christ, who opposes good to evil, is our true Mother. We have our being from him, where the foundation of motherhood begins, with all the sweet protection of love which endlessly follows."[9] Just as we are given birth and life by our natural mothers, Jesus Christ gives the Christian new birth and new life through his cross. Hence, she said, "And so Jesus is our true Mother in nature by our first creation, and he is our true Mother in grace by his taking our created nature. All the lovely works and all the sweet loving offices of beloved motherhood are appropriated to the second Person [of the Trinity], for in him we have this godly will, whole and safe forever, both in nature and grace, from his own goodness proper to him."[10]

Julian was also able to contrast natural motherhood with the supernatural "Motherhood" of Jesus Christ: "We know that all our mothers bear us for pain and for death. O, what is that? But our true Mother Jesus, he alone bears us for joy and for endless life, blessed may he be. So he carries us within him in love and travail, until the time when he wanted to suffer the sharpest thorns and cruel pain that ever were or will be, and at the last he died."[11]

Jesus is like our earthly mothers in a third way: "He feeds us with Himself." Just as our mothers fed us at their breast, Jesus feeds us from his Word and with his Supper. Hence, Julian wrote,

The mother can give her child to suck of her milk, but our precious Mother Jesus can feed us with himself, and does, most courteously and most tenderly, with the blessed sacrament, which is the precious food of true life; and with all the sweet sacraments he sustains us most mercifully and graciously, and so he meant in these blessed words, where he said: I am he Whom Holy Church preaches and teaches to you. That is to say: All the health and the life of the sacraments, all the power and the grace of my Word, all the goodness which is ordained in Holy Church for you, I am he."[12]

Motherhood meant so much to Julian that she could think of no bet-ter way to communicate the loving, selfless, protective care that she knew God in Jesus Christ has for God's children. She explained, "This fair lovely word 'mother' is so sweet and so kind in itself that it cannot truly be said of anyone or to anyone except of him and to him who is the true Mother of life and of all things."[13] Just as our mothers grew and nurtured us into becoming good, responsible, and mature people, so also the constancy of our heavenly Mother is seen in a love that grows us into spiritually mature Christians:

The kind, loving mother who knows and sees the need of her child guards it very tenderly, as the nature and condition of motherhood will have. And always as the child grows in age and in stature, she acts differently, but she does not change her love. And when it is even older, she allows it to be chastised to destroy its faults, so as to make the child receive virtues and grace. This work, with everything that is lovely and good, our Lord performs in those by whom it is done. So he is our Mother in nature by the operation of grace in the lower part, for love of the higher part.[14]

Julian's picture of God as "our true Mother" reminds us poignantly of the life-giving, nurturing, feeding, and protecting aspects of God. She was not concerned with the gender of God but rather with using homey, fam-ily-oriented theological metaphors that would fill the human heart with a profound sense of God's parental care for us. Just as our mother gives us life and cares for us from birth to adulthood, so also God gives us life (as well as new life in Christ), cares for us, and grows us into Christian maturity. In motherhood Julian found experience-laden metaphors for thinking and talking about God that communicated God's love power-fully to a world that desperately needed to hear the message of God's love.

Prayer

God, help me see you as an always loving Parent. Help me sense your acceptance and your life-giving power. Thank you for growing me into the person I am becoming through your grace in Jesus Christ and for the fruit of your Holy Spirit that you are growing in me. Help me not to be too complacent or too impatient with my growth as your child. Where I have failed to be the sort of person you would have me to be, let me start again; help me start afresh. Help me to see myself as you see me: full of talent, full of potential, full of the future. Help me also to see others with your loving eyes. In Jesus' name I pray. **Amen.**

Questions for Reflection

1. Why do you think Julian's message was so cherished and appreciated by Christians of her time and thereafter?

2. What do you think of Julian's willingness to draw on images and metaphors from her own life to help her understand and express her relationship with Jesus Christ? How do you react to her willingness to think about Jesus as "Our True Mother"?
3. In what specific ways is God (or Jesus) like a Mother (or Father) to us?

4. What images or metaphors—drawn from your own life or from the Bible—help you understand and express the relationship between God and God's people?

5. Are you able to draw strength and encouragement from the thought that God loves you with a Mother's love and wants the best for you and for your life? Why or why not?

6. How does God act like a Mother or a Parent toward us in the process of growing us into being the people God wants us to be?

Suggestions for Further Reading

Julian of Norwich: Showings, edited by Edmund Colledge and James Walsh (Paulist Press, 1978).

"Julian of Norwich," by Edmund G. Gardner, in *The Catholic Encyclopedia*, Vol. VIII (Robert Appelton Company, 1910). Also available at: http://www.newadvent.org/cathen/08557a.htm.

Julian of Norwich: Mystic and Theologian, by Grace M. Jantzen (Paulist Press, 1988).

Notes

[1] From *Julian of Norwich: Mystic and Theologian*, by Grace M. Jantzen (Paulist Press, 1988); pages 3–15.

[2] From *Christianity in the West, 1400–1700*, by John Bossy (Oxford University Press, 1987); pages 3–88.

[3] From "Julian of Norwich," by Elizabeth Spearing, in *The Literary Encyclopedia*. See http://www.litencyc.com/php/speople.php?rec=true&UID=5187.

[4] From *Julian of Norwich: Showings*, edited by James Colledge and James Walsh (Paulist Press, 1978); pages 129–130.

[5] From *Julian of Norwich: Showings*; page 130.

[6] From *Julian of Norwich: Showings*; page 130.

[7] From *Julian of Norwich: Showings*; page 131.

[8] From *Julian of Norwich: Showings*; page 293.

[9] From *Julian of Norwich: Showings*; page 295.

[10] From *Julian of Norwich: Showings*; pages 296–297.

[11] From *Julian of Norwich: Showings*; pages 297–298.

[12] From *Julian of Norwich: Showings*; page 298.

[13] From *Julian of Norwich: Showings*; pages 298–299.

[14] From *Julian of Norwich: Showings*; page 299.

IX

Martin Luther
(ca. 1483–1546)

Justification by Faith

Some people are very difficult to please. They are more apt to correct, criticize, or complain than they are to congratulate and affirm. Even when we try to please them with gifts or kindness, approval is not forthcoming.

Some people feel this way in their relationship with God. *God is perfect, and I am not,* they think to themselves. *Because of my imperfections, God judges me and condemns me. The only thing I can do to please God is to keep working harder at being a better person.*

This turns the freedom that is ours through Christian faith into an arduous sense of duty and a pattern of falling short and disappointing God. This is how Martin Luther felt before he discovered what it means to be justified by faith.

* * * *

The candles burned late into the night in the tower room of the Augustinian monastery in Wittenberg, Germany, as Dr. Martin Luther pored over piles of books. He was developing lectures for his university classes on the apostle Paul's Letter to the Romans. It must have seemed that a series of miracles had brought him to this place and time in his life. Born the son of a poor miner, he had received an excellent education. His father intended for Martin to become a lawyer so that he could take care of his parents in their later years. The law did not agree with Martin, however. As he was finishing his collegiate work, he found his vocational direction changed by a hasty vow he made while caught in open country during a booming thunderstorm. With lightning crashing all around him, Luther cried out, "Saint Anne, if you save me, I will become a monk."

It is understandable that young Martin Luther was frightened by the thought of death when he was caught in that thunderstorm. Death was very much on the minds of most late medieval people. Popular sermons and church artwork focused on death, and death had recently come quite close to Martin: One of his college friends had died by slipping and falling on the dagger that he carried in his boot as he was walking across open country.

It is also understandable as that young Martin was concerned about his eternal destiny in the midst of his reflection on death. He had been a spiritually anxious person ever since he was a young child. He was anxious in his relationship with his parents. He never seemed to be able to please them or to receive their praise. This sense of a lack of acceptance appeared to carry over to young Martin Luther's religious life as well. The Church of his day taught, more or less, that God helped those who helped themselves. The "good Christian" was the person who performed the myriad religious duties and observances that Church law and medieval custom required. If people did their very best, God would meet all their strivings with grace and grant them acceptance.

Martin Luther always felt uncertain, however, because he was never sure he had done his very best. Had he prayed enough? Had he attended the Church and her sacraments faithfully enough? Had he confessed *all* his sins, or were there some he had forgotten? So in the midst of this ongoing state of spiritual anxiety and in the face of what he thought was impending death, young Martin Luther cried out to his patron saint, Saint Anne (the mother of Mary the mother of Jesus), who reputedly offered special protection to miners. He begged for her help.

That Luther did not call out to God or to Jesus Christ and direct his vow to them was typical of the piety of the times. Most people felt so far from God that layers of saints and other intermediaries were used to approach God. Jesus Christ, who truly is our supreme way and access to the presence of God, was seen as a celestial tattletale who reported our shortcomings to God. In popular opinion, God was regarded as an angry Judge who was more apt to punish us for our sins than to forgive and receive us by divine grace. So young Martin Luther cried out to Saint Anne and made a vow to her that he would spend his life in service to the Church if she would spare his life. His life was spared, and he became a monk.

When Martin Luther entered the Augustinian monastery in July of 1505, he renounced worldly things and worldly people. He sold most of his possessions, gave a dinner party for his college friends, and then turned his back on the world in pursuit of peace with God.

Martin threw himself into the life of a monk with reckless abandon. He prayed, fasted, and studied far more than was required. Yet he still felt that God did not accept him or his acts of repentance and devotion. It was like his relationship with his earthly father all over again: never a word of acceptance, no kindly "well done," just more demands and more obligations. The harder Martin Luther worked at his monastic disciplines, the more anxious and more depressed he became. What was supposed to be the prescription for what ailed him had become instead another source of defeat and anxiety. As he would subsequently write, "Though I lived as a monk without reproach, I felt that I was a sinner before God with an extremely disturbed conscience."[1]

Luther's monastic supervisors recognized his spiritual struggles and refused to give him care of a congregation. Capitalizing on his prodigious intellectual abilities, they sent him for advanced theological training.

This was the path that brought Martin Luther, the Augustinian monk, to Wittenberg University as a doctoral student in Bible, a preacher at Saint Mary's Church, and a teacher to the undergraduates. It was in that last role that we find him in his study, poring over his books late into the night. He was struggling over one phrase in Romans 1:17. Luther explained,

> I had indeed been captivated with an extraordinary ardor for understanding Paul in the Epistle to the Romans. But up till then it was not the cold blood about the heart, but the single word in Chapter 1 [:17], "In it the righteousness of God is revealed," that stood in my way. For I hated that word "righteousness of God," which, according to the use and custom of all the teachers, I had been taught to understand philosophically regarding the formal or active righteousness, as they called it, with which God is righteous and punishes the unrighteous sinner.[2]

Reaching back through his years in the monastery and beyond, Martin Luther had been troubled by this understanding of "the righteousness of

God." It had been a recurring source of pain and spiritual bondage for him. He recalled,

> I did not love, yes, I hated the righteous God who punishes sinners, and secretly, if not blasphemously, certainly murmuring greatly, I was angry with God and said, "As if, indeed, it is not enough, that miserable sinners, eternally lost through original sin, are crushed by every kind of calamity by the law of the decalogue, without having God add pain to pain by the gospel and also by the gospel threatening us with his righteousness and wrath!" Thus I raged with a fierce and troubled conscience. Nevertheless, I beat importunately upon Paul at that place, most ardently desiring to know what St. Paul wanted.[3]

As Luther boldly, angrily, and prayerfully wrestled with the text of Romans, the light of God's grace—the true meaning of the passage about "the righteousness of God"—dawned on him:

> At last, by the mercy of God, meditating day and night, I gave heed to the context of the words, namely, "In it the righteousness of God is revealed, as it is written, 'He who through faith is righteous shall live.'" There I began to understand that the righteousness of God is that by which the righteousness of God is revealed by the gospel, namely, the passive righteousness with which merciful God justifies us by faith, as it is written, "He who through faith is righteous shall live."[4]

This was a tremendous breakthrough in Martin Luther's understanding of God; it meant that he was coming to see God no longer as One who primarily judges and punishes sinners, but rather as One who provides sinners with justification through their faith in Jesus Christ. Rather than being a message of condemnation and destruction, "the righteousness of God" now became for Martin Luther a message of justification and acceptance before God.

Luther experienced a tremendous sense of freedom and exuberant relief because of this new realization. As he later described it, "Here I felt that I was altogether born again and had entered paradise itself through open gates. There a totally other ["new"] face of the entire Scripture showed itself to me. Thereupon I ran through the Scriptures from memory. I also found in other terms an analogy, as, the work of God, that is, what God does in us, the power of God, with which he makes us strong, the wisdom of God, with which he makes us wise, the strength of God, the salvation of God, the glory of God."[5]

The very concept that had held Martin Luther in spiritual bondage became, when properly understood and embraced, the key to his spiritual freedom. Hence, Luther wrote, "I extolled my sweetest word with a love as great as the hatred with which I had before hated the word 'righteousness of God.' Thus that place in Paul was for me truly the gate to paradise."[6]

Martin Luther subsequently returned to the topic of righteousness in his sermon on "Two Kinds of Righteousness" (1519). In delineating the two kinds of righteousness, Luther showed the effect of his "Tower Experience" and the new understanding of God he gained from it. He proclaimed,

> There are two kinds of Christian righteousness, just as man's sin is of two kinds.
> The first is *alien righteousness*, that is the righteousness of another, instilled from without. This is the righteousness of Christ by which he justifies through faith, as it is written in 1 Cor. 1[:30]: "Whom God made our wisdom, our righteousness and sanctification and redemption." In John 11[:25-26], Christ himself states: "I am the resurrection and the life; he who believes in me...shall never die."...This righteousness, then, is given to men in baptism and whenever they are truly repentant. Therefore a man can with confidence boast in Christ and say: "Mine are Christ's living, doing, and speaking, his suffering, and dying, mine as much as if I had lived, done, spoken, suffered, and died as he did."[7]

This "alien righteousness" is the righteousness of our Lord Jesus Christ, which was manifested in his holy life and sacrificial death. By faith in Jesus Christ's death and resurrection, this "alien righteousness"—which is Christ's and not our own—is given to us for our acceptance (justification) before God. As Luther explained, "Through faith in Christ, therefore, Christ's righteousness becomes our righteousness and all that he has becomes ours; rather, he himself becomes ours."[8]

The second kind of righteousness with which a Christian concerns himself or herself, Luther called "proper righteousness." He wrote, "The second kind of righteousness is our *proper righteousness*, not because we alone work it, but because we work with that first and alien righteousness. This is that manner of life spent profitably in good works, in the first place, in slaying the flesh and crucifying the desires with respect to the self....In the second place, this righteousness consists in love to one's neighbor, and in the third place, in meekness and fear ["reverence"] toward God."[9]

Where Martin Luther had previously thought that a person was accepted and saved by God through her or his "proper righteousness" (the good deeds that she or he did), he had—after his "Tower Experience"—come to see that a person is saved and justified before God only by "alien righteousness" (the merits of Jesus Christ that are received by faith). Luther had been trying to place the "cart before the horse." He had been trying to do good works to please God before he had been saved, accepted, and transformed by faith in Jesus Christ. Now he had come to see these two kinds of righteousness in a more-appropriate way.

Faith in Christ bestows on us the righteousness whereby we are saved and accepted before God. Out of this relationship of faith, love, and acceptance, the Christian learns to do good works, which not only please God but also serve to increase our holiness and help our neighbors. Or as Luther would later (in 1520) stress in his treatise *On Christian Freedom,*

> Our faith in Christ does not free us from works but from false opinions concerning works, that is, from the foolish presumption that justification is acquired by works. Faith redeems, corrects, and preserves our consciences so that we know that righteousness does not consist in works, although works neither can nor ought to be wanting; just as we cannot be without food and drink and all the works of this mortal body, yet our righteousness is not in them, but in faith; and yet those works of the body are not to be despised or neglected on that account.[10]

The discovery of a gracious God behind the doctrine of justification by faith (and not works) was the heart of Martin Luther's experience in the tower. It set him free from the bondage of an anxious and burdened conscience and from looking on his Christian faith as a path of duty that must be followed and obligations that must be fulfilled in order to please God. After his tower experience, Luther lived with a profound sense of Christian freedom. He trusted in Christ for his justification and resolved to live in a free and spontaneous love for God and neighbor.

Luther's discovery of justification by faith caused him to pen the "Ninety-Five Theses" in October 1517—in protest of the Church promising forgiveness in exchange for financial contributions—and thereby set off the chain of events that became the Protestant Reformation. But the larger, world-shaking reformation began more modestly than one might think. It began with the reformation of one person's understanding of the righteousness of God and with the relief that came to his troubled conscience when he looked to Jesus Christ for his salvation instead of to his own good deeds and best efforts.

This is where Luther's witness touches each of us. It reminds us that we can never do enough to earn God's approval and that it is foolish for us to think of our lives in ways that keep us trying to work harder, do more, and be better on our own. There are no deals or "plea bargains" to be cut with God. Works righteousness always fails and frustrates in the end. But God has provided us with a better and more-liberating way, the "alien right-eousness" of Jesus Christ that becomes ours through faith in Christ. This is a liberating and transforming kind of faith that takes the duty out of good works and impels us toward doing good out of a deep sense of gratitude for what God has already done for us in Jesus Christ.

Prayer

Faithful and righteous God, I thank you that your Son has done for me what I could not do for myself. I thank you for the awareness that I do not have to work my way into your heart and acceptance. Thank you that I can be certain of your acceptance and approval through the righteousness of your Son and that I can live my life freely and spontaneously in Christ without a morbid sense of duty weighing down my thoughts and actions. In Jesus' name I pray. **Amen.**

Questions for Reflection

1. Would you characterize your Christian pilgrimage as one of freedom or as one of duty?

2. What insights did you gain from Luther's understanding of alien righteousness and proper righteousness? How did his understanding of the relationship of these two kinds of righteousness affect his inner state and Christian faith? How might it affect yours?

3. How do contemporary Christians sometimes get caught up in a theology of salvation by works? How can we avoid this?

4. How might we maintain a clearer sense of our freedom and spontaneity in Jesus Christ?

5. How do you understand the role of good works in Christian life and faith?

For Further Reading

Here I Stand: A Life of Martin Luther, by Roland Bainton (Abingdon Press, 1955), various reprints.

Martin Luther: Selections From His Writings, edited by John Dillenberger (Anchor Books, 1958).

Notes

[1] From *Luther's Works*, edited by Louis W. Spitz, Vol. 34 (Muhlenberg Press, 1960); page 336.

[2] From *Luther's Works*, edited by Louis Spitz, Vol. 34; page 336.

[3] From *Luther's Works*, edited by Louis Spitz, Vol. 34; pages 336–337.

[4] From *Luther's Works*, edited by Louis Spitz, Vol. 34; page 337.

[5] From *Luther's Works*, edited by Louis Spitz, Vol. 34; page 337.

[6] From *Luther's Works*, edited by Louis Spitz, Vol. 34; page 337.

[7] From *Luther's Works*, edited by Harold J. Grim, Vol. 31 (Fortress Press, 1957); page 297. Emphasis added.

[8] From *Luther's Works*, edited by Harold J. Grim, Vol. 31; page 298.

[9] From *Luther's Works*, edited by Harold J. Grim, Vol 31; page 299. Emphasis added.

[10] From "The Freedom of a Christian," in *Luther's Works*, edited by Harold J. Grim, Vol. 31; pages 372–373.

X

John Calvin
(1509–1564)

God's Providence

The writer of Proverbs reports, "The human mind plans the way, but the LORD directs the steps" (Proverbs 16:9). Do you think that God directs our steps? John Calvin certainly did. He had the faith to see God at work in the events in his life, and he struggled to be faithful when he felt God calling him to new and greater opportunities for Christian service.

* * * *

John Calvin was born in Noyon, France. He grew up in the shadow of the great Gothic cathedral where his father was a lawyer at the ecclesiastical court. Calvin's father was a fiercely ambitious, self-made man who had risen to prominence as the financial agent for the local bishop. John's mother died when he was a boy, and her absence from his life probably contributed to his shy and retiring personality.

In 1521, when Calvin was twelve, his father used his ecclesiastical connections to arrange for young John to receive an appointment as a chaplain at one of the altars in the cathedral. No one expected a twelve-year-old boy to say Mass and offer prayers at the altar; this was a convenient way to use the funds from an endowed ministry to pay for his educational expenses. Calvin's father had decided that John would become a priest. Young Calvin warmed to the idea and went off to study at the University of Paris (which was also called "the Sorbonne").

Calvin's Parisian interlude was one of the happiest times of his life. Then as now, Paris was an exciting place to visit. It was a hotbed of new thinking and new religious ideas. While the theological tenor of the University of Paris was conservative Roman Catholic—its theological faculty had declared Martin Luther a heretic in 1520—the intellectual climate of the city was progressive. Several of Europe's leading Renaissance scholars were in residence there; and true to the dictum of their movement, *Ad Fontes!* (Latin: "To the Sources"), these men were studying the Bible directly from the original languages, as well as teaching and preaching it in the French vernacular. Calvin's cousin, Peter Olivetan, was a fledgling Bible scholar; and he introduced John Calvin to the leading figures in the field.

Among John's new friends was Nicholas Cop. Cop was an exemplary "Renaissance man" who held degrees in law and philosophy. He was also a Protestant sympathizer who had two sons approximately the same age as John Calvin. Calvin became a frequent visitor in Cop's home. Young John grew to manhood studying theology at the University of Paris and studying the Bible with the leading linguists of his day.

In 1528, John Calvin's happy life in Paris took an abrupt and unexpected turn. His father was dismissed from his lucrative position at the cathedral and excommunicated from the Roman Catholic Church for unspecified abuses of his office. Most commentators assume that the elder Calvin had misappropriated some of the bishop's funds; whatever the crime, its effect on the younger Calvin was clear. His father, out of utter distaste for the Church, withdrew John from theological studies and insisted that he pursue a career in the law instead. Writing in 1557, John recalled,

> When I was as yet a very little boy, my father had destined me for the study of theology. But afterwards, when he considered that the legal profession commonly raised those who followed it to wealth, this prospect induced him suddenly to change his purpose. Thus it came to pass, that I was withdrawn from the study of philosophy, and was put to the study of law. To this pursuit I endeavoured faithfully to apply myself, in obedience to the will of my father; but God, by the *secret guidance of His providence*, at length gave a different direction to my course.[1]

From 1528–1533, John Calvin studied the law, first at Bourges and then at Orleans—among the finest schools available. While many biographers find a correlation between the rational complexion of legal studies and Calvin's orderly mind and temperament, the rigors of legal studies did not wear well on him. He developed ulcers, insomnia, and other illnesses from studying too long and too hard on a course of inquiry that seemed useless to him. He was providentially released from this rigorous path of frustration by the death of his father, which came in 1533. No longer obligated to follow his father's wishes, John was now free to pursue his own course of action; and he promptly returned to his former, happier life in Paris.

God's providential intervention in John Calvin's life continued as he was led to an evangelical (gospel-centered) conversion sometime between 1529 and 1533. As he subsequently wrote,

> Since I was too obstinately devoted to the superstitions of Popery to be easily extricated from so profound an abyss of mire, God by a sudden conversion subdued and brought my mind to a teachable frame, which was more hardened in such matters than might have been expected from one at my early period of life. Having thus received some taste and knowledge of true godliness, I was immediately inflamed with so intense a desire to make progress therein, that although I did not altogether leave off other studies, I yet pursued them with less ardour.[2]

This "sudden conversion," while described in singularly unemotional terms, was none the less deep and profound. It was from the standpoint of his post-conversion faith that Calvin was able to see the hand of God guiding and shaping his life in those early years in ways that he did not recognize at the time.

John Calvin would later describe God's providence in his monumental *Institutes of the Christian Religion*. Just as certainly as God was Creator of the world, so God was to be viewed as the Governor and Preserver of the same:

> Not only in that he drives the celestial frame as well as its several parts by a universal motion, but also in that he sustains, nourishes, and cares for, everything he has made, even to the last sparrow [cf. Matt. 10:29]. Thus, David, having briefly stated that the universe was created by God, immediately descends to the uninterrupted course of His providence. "By the word of Jehovah the heavens were made, and all their host by the breath of his mouth"

[Ps. 33:6...]. Soon thereafter he adds, "Jehovah has looked down on the sons of men" [Ps. 33:13...], and what follows is in the same vein. For although all men do not reason so clearly, yet,...it would not be believable that human affairs are cared for by God unless he were the Maker of the universe, and nobody seriously believes the universe was made by God without being persuaded that he takes care of his works.[3]

Thus, Calvin believed that God, as Supreme Creator, was also Governor, Preserver, and Director of the universe. Calvin had no place in his theology for "good luck." Or as he described it, "That this difference may better appear, we must know that God's providence, as it is taught in Scripture, is opposed to fortune and fortuitous happenings."[4] Hence, he urged, "At the outset, then, let my readers grasp that providence means not that by which God idly observes from heaven what takes place on earth, but that by which, as keeper of the keys, he governs all events."[5] For John Calvin, "Providence" means that God does not sit on the sidelines of human history, perhaps rooting for the "good guys" and the "good gals" or good outcomes. God intervenes in history with the force of God's will and Holy Spirit to cause things to work towards "the Good." Because evil has been set loose in the world in the person of Satan and because humans make free and fallible choices, it is not possible to say that everything that happens in the world is consistent with God's plan or is a product of God's will. It does mean that God joins us at work in the world as we strive for good and godly ends.

John Calvin learned to see God's providence at work in the lives of the heroes of the Bible. In the Hebrew Scriptures, Joseph was a notable example. His brothers kidnapped Joseph and sold him into slavery in Egypt. While being a faithful and God-fearing slave in Egypt, Joseph was imprisoned because the wife of his master (Potiphar) falsely charged him with sexual improprieties. In prison Joseph remained faithful to God and used his gift for interpreting dreams to help two fellow inmates. One of these men returned to Pharaoh's favor and arranged to have Joseph released from prison so that he could interpret Pharaoh's troubling dreams. By accurately interpreting Pharaoh's dreams, Joseph was able to save Egypt from terrible ruin and starvation. In reward for his service Pharaoh made Joseph his right-hand man, second ruler over all of Egypt.

When Joseph's Hebrew family visited Egypt to buy food during the time of starvation, Joseph was reunited with his relatives. And more importantly, he was able to see all these events that had lead to his rise to power in Egypt as a part of God's providential plan. As Joseph told his brothers in Genesis 45:7-8, "God sent me before you to preserve for you a remnant on earth, and to keep alive for you many survivors. So it was not you who sent me here, but God; he has made me a father to Pharaoh, and lord of all his house and ruler over the land of Egypt." Joseph's brothers may have meant his kidnapping and captivity for evil, but God was able to use them for good. Commenting on Genesis 45:8, Calvin wrote, "This is a remark-able passage, in which we are taught that the right course of events is never so disturbed by the depravity and wickedness of men, but that God can direct them to a good end. We are also instructed in what manner and for what purpose we must consider the providence of God"[6]

Romans 8:28 communicates the same message: "We know that all things work together for good for those who love God, who are called according to his purpose." Commenting on this passage of Scripture, Calvin wrote, "It is certain that Paul notes the order, so that we may know that the fact that everything happens to the saints for their salvation depends on the free adoption of God as the first cause."[7]

Through Bible passages like these, Calvin learned to expect and to see God's hand at work in his life even in those situations that did not seem to be happy or pleasant to him or helpful in the pursuit of his own plans. John Calvin's life did not immediately run smoothly after his conversion, however.

Calvin returned to Paris and his studies there, and by 1532 he had pub-lished his first book—A Commentary on Seneca's De Clementia. It was exactly the sort of work to be expected from the Renaissance scholar he hoped to become. Also in 1532, his friend Nicholas Cop was invited to become rector of the University of Paris. His inaugural speech, given on All Saints' Day of that year, rebuked the learned doctors of the Sorbonne from the standpoint of criticisms leveled at the Church by Martin Luther and others. Calvin is thought to have had a hand in the speech. Whether or not that is true, Nicholas Cop's inaugural speech expressed many Protestant-like ideas.

It soon became dangerous to harbor Reformation ideas in Roman Catholic Paris. Calvin went home to Lyon to resign his chaplaincies and relinquish the funds associated with them. His homefolks repaid him with a stint in jail, after which he fled to the south of France. There he began to hold clandestine Protestant meetings. Still hoping to satisfy his scholarly longings, Calvin retired to Basel in Switzerland, where he penned the first edition of his famous *Institutes of the Christian Religion* in 1536.

Later in 1536, while traveling to Strasburg, in Germany, John Calvin passed through Geneva, Switzerland. Little did he know that it would be the location of his greatest work.

William Farel had been trying, with little success, to start a Protestant church in Geneva when he met young John Calvin in a tavern there. The two men struck up a conversation, and soon Farel realized that Calvin was precisely the man he needed to help him bring Reformation ideas to Geneva. He urged John to join him in the work; but Calvin refused, offering a catalog of excuses: "Why should I be the one to help you? Can't you see...I am timid, weak, and fainthearted by nature, and feel myself not equal to such opposition?"[8]

Farel, however, was convinced that it was God's providence that brought Calvin to Geneva; and he was not going to let him go so easily. "If you refuse," he thundered, "...God will condemn you."[9] And so, sensing the hand of God in these events, Calvin capitulated. He later wrote, "I felt God had reached down from heaven and laid his hand on me with force."[10]

Calvin's Herculean reform labors, which had the result of beginning the Reformed or Calvinist tradition, were a terrible burden to him, however: "This I can honestly testify: not a day passed in which I did not long for death ten times."[11] Writing to Farel, Calvin said, "Had I the choice at my own disposal, nothing would be less agreeable to me than to follow your advice. But when I remember that I am not my own, I offer up my heart, a slain victim for a sacrifice to the Lord...I submit my will and my affections subdued and held fast to the obedience of God."[12] As a result, he established a great church in Geneva; and a significant Protestant religious tradition was born.

John Calvin did not believe in luck. He believed in God's providence. He viewed the events of his life from the standpoint of his Christian faith, and from this perspective he came to see that God does indeed direct our steps. When confronted with a call to Christian service, Calvin regarded that challenge as an opportunity for growth and service that came to him from God. Calvin was obedient to the call even though it ran against the grain of his own plans and inclinations.

Prayer

Providential God, please help me see your hand at work in my life. Direct my steps so that I may serve you more effectively. Help me see life's challenges as opportunities for greater spiritual growth and greater service to you. In Christ's name I pray. **Amen.**

Questions for Reflection

1. Reflect on Genesis 45:7-8 and Romans 8:28. What do they say to you about God's providence? How do you see God's hand at work in your life?

2. Can you think of an instance in which circumstances have offered you an opportunity for greater Christian growth or service? If so, did you say "Yes" to that opportunity? Why or why not?

3. Do you find comfort in the promise that God is able to bring good out of challenging circumstances when people seek to follow God's will? How might this insight affect your Christian life?

4. What challenging circumstances are you facing? Do you feel that God is at work in them? Have you asked for God's help in resolving these issues in accordance with his will?

For Further Reading

"John Calvin," by B.A. Gerrish, in *Reformers in Profile* (Wipf and Stock, 2004).

Calvin's Institutes of the Christian Religion (abridged), edited by Tony Lane and Hilary Osborn (Baker Books Academic, 1987).

A Life of John Calvin, by Alister McGrath (Blackwells Publishing House, 1993).

Notes

[1] From *Commentary on the Book of Psalms*, by John Calvin, translated by James Anderson (William B. Eerdmans Publishing Company, 1949); Vol. I, xl. Emphasis added.

[2] From *Commentary on the Book of Psalms*; Vol. I, xl–xli.

[3] From *Calvin: Institutes of the Christian Religion*, 2 Vol., edited by John T. McNeill (The Westminster Press, 1960); I:197–198.

[4] From *Calvin: Institutes of the Christian Religion*, 2 Vol., edited by John T. McNeill; I:198.

[5] From *Calvin: Institutes of the Christian Religion*, 2 Vol., edited by John T. McNeill; I:201–202.

[6] From *Commentaries on the First Book of Moses Called Genesis*, by John Calvin, 2 Vol., translated by John King (William B. Eerdmans Publishing Co., 1948); II:377.

[7] From *Calvin's Commentaries: The Epistles of Paul the Apostle to the Romans and to the Thessalonians*, translated by Ross Mackenzie (William B. Eerdmans Publishing Co., 1960); pages 179–180.

[8] From *Calvin*, by Emanuel Stickelberger (James Clarke & Co., 1959); page 47.

[9] From *The History and Character of Calvinism*, by John T. McNeil (Oxford University Press, 1954, 1973); page 136.

[10] From *Four Reformers*, by Kurt Aland (Augsburg Publishing House, 1979); page 104.

[11] From *Reformers in Profile*, edited by B.A. Gerish (Fortress Press, 1967); page 147.

[12] From *Calvin: Geneva and the Reformation*, by Ronald S. Wallace (Baker Book House, 1988); page 24.

XI

John and Charles Wesley
(1703–1791)

Holiness of Heart and Life

One of the truisms about human nature is that we become what we love. People who love money become increasingly materialistic. People who love violent pastimes often find violence creeping into their lives. People become like the people they love. Over time "old married couples" are able to complete each other's sentences. And if we are to believe what we see on television programs like "America's Funniest Home Videos," some people even begin to resemble their pets—or vice versa.

But what about those of us who profess to love a holy God? Should we expect to become more holy as a result of whom we love? This certainly seems to be God's will for us. As the Bible says, "You shall be holy, for I the LORD your God am holy" (Leviticus 19:2). In a similar way, Jesus urged, "Be perfect, therefore, as your heavenly Father is perfect" (Matthew 5:48).

John and Charles Wesley had a profound passion for Christian holiness. Christian holiness was a vision and a goal that captured their imaginations and fueled the fire of their faith over the course of their lives.

* * * *

The Wesley brothers first learned about holiness of heart and life at their mother's knee—as Susanna Wesley taught them to read from the Bible, to say their prayers, and to examine their consciences. In their father's study the boys learned theology, Greek, Latin, and logic; but from their mother they learned the practical piety that would shape their hopes and aspirations throughout their lives. When they were away at college, both John and Charles Wesley wrote to their father, Samuel, when they had questions about theology. But they wrote to their mother about their spiritual struggles and questions of faith.

At Oxford University the Wesleys earned "the harmless name of a Methodist" for themselves by attending the weekly observance of the Lord's Supper and following "the method of [devotional] study prescribed by the statutes of the University."[1] Soon a small group of devout and earnest students formed around the Wesleys. Under John's direction these students became the Oxford Holy Club. It was typical that the friendliness and buoyant personality of Charles Wesley got the group started and John Wesley's organizational skills gave it shape and direction.

Their reading of the Greek New Testament and the early church fathers set the Oxford Methodists on a regimen of spiritual disciplines and good deeds that was aimed at producing sanctification (From the Latin: *sanctus*, "being made holy"). They not only devoured devotional classics like Thomas a` Kempis' *Imitation of Christ*, they also strove to carry out the Christian practices they read about there. John Wesley reported that in 1726 he had read a` Kempis' "Christian Pattern." It taught him "the nature and extent of inward religion." Hence he wrote, "The religion of the heart now appeared to me in a stronger light than ever it had done before." John continued, "I saw, that 'simplicity of intention, and purity of affection,' one design in all we speak or do, and one desire ruling all our tempers, are indeed 'the wings of the soul,' without which she can never ascend to the mount of God."[2]

The Oxford Methodists also read William Law's *Practical Treatise on Christian Perfection*. John Wesley said that Law's treatise "convinced [him], more than ever, of the absolute impossibility of being half a Christian."[3] Based on his reading of Law, Wesley came to the realization that holiness was not simply a pattern of good deeds or moral virtues. Christian holiness amounted to an utter transformation of the inner person. Studying Law's treatise gave the Methodists the impetus to strive for "Christian perfection."

Reading the New Testament also profoundly shaped the Wesleys' understanding of holiness and Christian perfection. John Wesley wrote, "In the year 1729, I began not only to read, but to study, the Bible as the one, the only standard of truth, and pure religion." In doing so, the Wesley brothers came to see that "conformity to our Master" was the essential nature of true Christianity. John reported, "I generally considered religion, as a uniform following of Christ, an entire inward and outward conformity to our Master."[4]

The Wesleys insisted on using Bible words to describe Bible doctrines, so the terminology they used to describe holiness of heart and life came straight from the Bible. Their terminology was shaped and hammered out by reflection on biblical texts such as the following: "Be perfect therefore, as your heavenly Father is perfect" (Matthew 5:48); "Let us go on toward perfection" (Hebrews 6:1, combined with Hebrews 13:20-21): "Now may the God of peace...make you complete in everything good so that you may do his will." These passages were connected with statements like those in 1 John 3:9: "Those who have been born of God do not sin" and 1 John 4:18: "There is no fear in love, but perfect love casts out fear." In these instances, and many others we could point to in the Greek New Testament, the English word *perfect* stands for a word from the *telos* family in New Testament Greek.

These words carry the connotation of being made "whole," "complete," or "mature." Hence, the holiness of heart and life that Christian perfection describes is being "whole" (not divided) and "mature" in our Christian thoughts and attitudes. It is being made "complete" by the renewing work of God that Christian faith begins in the inner person. It is the establishment of "the same mind...that was in Christ Jesus" (Philippians 2:5) within a person through an invasion of the Holy Spirit and an infusion of God's love.

After college, John and Charles Wesley both went on missionary adventures to Georgia, in the American South. Both brothers failed to live up to their own expectations with respect to the effectiveness and success of their Georgia ministries. They returned to England full of questions about their own spiritual state, as well as with doubts about their effectiveness as ministers. John's journal entry for January 24, 1738 expressed his inner turmoil: "I went to America to convert the Indians but, oh, who shall convert me? Who, what, is he that will deliver me from this evil heart of unbelief? I have a fair summer religion. I can talk well, nay, and believe myself, while no danger is near. But let me look death in the face, and my spirit is troubled. Nor can I say [with St. Paul], 'to die is gain.' "[5]

In May 1738, after the depressing failure of their Georgia missionary adventures, both Wesleys experienced dramatic conversions. Charles' conversion came while he was sick in bed. On May 21, one of his nurses urged him, "In the name of Jesus of Nazareth, arise, and believe, and thou shalt be healed of all thy infirmities."[6] Charles wrote in his journal that later that day, "I now found myself at peace with God."[7]

John Wesley's conversion occurred on May 24. John described the event this way: "In the evening, I went very unwillingly to a society [small-group meeting] in Aldersgate Street, where one was reading Luther's Preface to the Epistle to the Romans. About a quarter before nine, while he was describing the change which God works in the heart through faith in Christ, I felt my heart strangely warmed. I felt that I did trust in Christ, Christ alone for salvation; and an assurance was given me that He had taken away *my* sins, even *mine*, and saved *me* from the law of sin and death."[8]

Although the Wesleys had been preaching and striving for holiness of heart and life long before the dramatic events of May 1738, they had been doing so with a misapprehension about the nature of their acceptance before God. Prior to their conversions, the Wesleys thought that their standing before God was based on their ability to achieve holiness through their strivings; after their conversion experiences, however, they came to understand the Reformation doctrine of justification by faith. They came to see that holiness was the fruit and spiritual outcome of acceptance by God and *not* the basis of it. Three months after his conversion, Charles Wesley explained this important transition to his former mentor, William Law. "I told him," Charles wrote in his journal, "he was my schoolmaster to bring me to Christ; but the reason why I did not some sooner to Him, was, my seeking to be sanctified before I was justified."[9]

Almost immediately after his conversion experience, Charles Wesley began writing a hymn to express the fervor of his new understanding of faith. In fact, he wrote several hymns over the next few days. When his brother John came to visit him, fresh from his Aldersgate experience, they sang Charles' hymns together. These were among the first of the more than 9,000 hymns and sacred poems that Charles would write over the course of his busy ministry. They provide us with a vital window into his heart and mind.

One of the hymns that Charles wrote immediately after his conversion was "Free Grace." It was subsequently published in 1739. This hymn is more familiar to us when named by the phraseology of the author's first line: "And can it be, that I should gain." The first few verses, written in first-person form, give voice to the wonder and excitement that Charles found in God's grace, which was made available to him through faith in Jesus Christ. Hence he wrote, "Amazing love! How can it be / That Thou, my God, shouldst die for me?"[10] Verses four and five of the same hymn are replete with what have become standard Wesleyan salvation themes: The life of sin is likened to a sinful slumber. Justification by faith awakens a person from this slumber and sets her or him free from the guilt and power of sin. Justification leads directly to deliverance from sin and new birth.

New birth is the beginning of sanctification, in which the inner life of the person is reborn and renewed by the Holy Spirit. Deliverance from sin brings with it the witness of the Spirit, as "the still small voice" of God whispers the good news of divine acceptance in our hearts. The same invasion by the Holy Spirit not only cleanses the Christian's heart but also enables Christ to be present there:

> Long my imprison'd spirit lay,
>   Fast bound in sin and nature's night;
> Thine eye diffused a quickening ray;
>   I woke; the dungeon flamed with light;
> My chains fell off, my heart was free,
>   I rose, went forth, and follow'd thee.
>
> Still the small inward voice I hear,
>   That whispers all my sins forgiven;
> Still the atoning blood is near,
>   That quench'd the wrath of hostile heaven:
> I feel the life His wounds impart;
>   I feel my Saviour in my heart.[11]

Fully characteristic of the Wesley brothers was the fact that they promptly began proclaiming their newly found understanding of the relationship of justification and sanctification by faith. Soon multitudes were standing in public parks and graveyards, even in inclement weather, to hear them preach this good news. Equally characteristic of the Wesleys was the fact that they published an important book that reflected their reorientation of the doctrines of justification and sanctification. Somewhat surprising, however, is the fact that this book was a hymnal! It was theology written in a medium that ordinary people could readily use and understand. The Wesleys' jointly published *Hymns and Sacred Poems* (1739) was the immediate result of their discovery of justification and sanctification by faith.

In the "Preface" of that work they reported that they had leaned too heavily on the work of Christian mystics (like William Law), which had confused their earlier understanding of sanctification. They wrote, "The sole cause of our acceptance with God...is the righteousness and death of Christ, who fulfilled God's law, and died in our stead. And even the condition of it is not (as they suppose) our righteousness of heart or life; but our faith alone."[12]

This same "Preface" evidences a second important development: It describes how the Wesleys had come to understand the reception of holiness. Focusing their attention on Acts 2, they considered it "the gift of the Holy Ghost," which was directly connected to their "'fellowship and...breaking of bread,' and...praying [together] 'with one accord.'"[13] This realization, like their earlier experiences in the Oxford Holy Club, taught them that sanctification is learned in the context of small groups and through faith-filled attention to spiritual disciplines. This development was soon set to work in the formation of the Methodist movement. The Wesleys required that those people who had experienced spiritual awakening through their open-air evangelism and who wanted to be "a Methodist" become members of a Methodist Society and attend a weekly class meeting.

"The Rules of the United Societies" (also written in 1739) urged the members to desire to "flee from the wrath to come, to be saved from their sins." Therefore the early Methodists promised to "first...[do] no harm," such as swearing, breaking the sabbath, getting drunk, buying or selling liquors, brawling, and so forth. Second, they promised to "do good," both to the bodies and the souls of their neighbors, by "giving food to the hungry, by clothing the naked, by visiting or helping them that are sick, or in prison" and by "instructing, reproving, or exhorting" all people with whom they have connection—to the good of their souls. And third, the early Methodists promised to "[attend] upon all the ordinances of God." These "ordinances" were spiritual disciplines that included "the public worship of God; the ministry of the word, either read or expounded; the supper of the Lord; family and private prayer; searching the Scriptures; and fasting, or abstinence."[14]

The "Rules" of the Methodist Societies committed the early members to participation in small groups, the exercise of spiritual disciplines, and social activism as a direct and obvious response to justification by faith and their hunger for holiness. Not only did the Methodists seek to be saved from their past sins, they expected to be able to live free from the power of sin in their lives. As transformed people, they also expected to be able to transform the world by feeding the hungry, clothing the naked, and visiting the sick as they shared the gospel of Jesus Christ. Hence, the Wesleys' 1739 "Preface" urged, "The gospel of Christ knows of no religion, but social; no holiness but social holiness. 'Faith working by love' is the length and breadth and depth and height of Christian perfection."[15]

Soon thereafter Charles Wesley offered a description of this kind of "perfection" in his journal entry for Monday, September 26, 1740: It is "utter dominion over sin; constant peace, and love, and joy in the Holy Ghost; the full assurance of faith, righteousness, and true holiness."[16] The Wesleyan "minutes" from their annual conference of 1744 answered the question "What is implied in being a perfect Christian?" by answering, "The loving the Lord our God with all our heart, and with all our mind, and soul, and strength."[17] This kind of "perfect love" is the fulfillment of the greatest commandment:" "You shall love the Lord your God with all your heart, and with all your soul, and with all your strength, and with all your mind; and your neighbor as yourself" (Luke 10:27).

Christian concepts like "holiness" or "perfection" sound utterly unattainable for human beings. But what seems impossible with us is possible for God. Scriptural holiness is not about perfect moral performance; it is about utter dedication and consecration to God, a willingness consistently to put God first in our lives and to allow God to work his transforming will within us. In a similar way, "Christian perfection" is not getting a perfect score on the exam called "Christian Life." Perfection in the biblical sense is being "whole, mature, or complete." It means that our wills become so pliable to the will of God that we learn to will what God wills and to love what God loves. The infusion of God's love and the invasion of his Holy Spirit are instrumental in this process. It also means that perfection is not a standard of performance; it is wholehearted purity through consecration to God.

This is the kind of purity that jewelers have in mind when they tell us that the watch we are examining is "pure gold." They mean it is "unmixed"; there are no other alloys in the metal. Christian perfection, in this sense, is a purity of heart in which our lives are consecrated to God in undivided love and unmixed commitment.

Prayer

Lord, I know that you are a holy God and that you want me to be like you. You want me to will what you will and to love the things you love. Too often, it seems as if I am a walking civil war. I want what you want, but I want what I want too. Sometimes I want my will more than I want your will. Help me give myself over to you and place myself and the things I love totally in your hands. Give me a new heart so that I can love my neighbor as myself. In the powerful name of Jesus I pray. **Amen.**

Questions for Reflection

1. How do you understand what the Wesleys meant by "Christian perfection"? How would you describe the desire to love God with your whole heart and to love your neighbor as yourself?

2. What concerns or issues sometimes keep us from directing our attention toward God? toward our neighbor? How might God's love and transforming power help us overcome these barriers?

3. What role do good works like spiritual disciplines play in cultivating and developing a greater love for God and neighbor?

4. What spiritual disciplines did the Wesley brothers advocate? What spiritual disciplines do you practice? What spiritual disciplines might you practice?

5. Why did the Wesleys require all their followers to become members of a small group? How might a small group help Christians with their sanctification?

For Further Reading

A Real Christian: The Life of John Wesley, by Kenneth Collins (Abingdon Press, 1999).

John Wesley, edited by Albert Outler (Oxford University Press, 1980).

Charles Wesley: A Reader, edited by John R. Tyson (Oxford University Press, 1989).

Assist Me to Proclaim: The Life and Hymns of Charles Wesley, by John R. Tyson (William B. Eerdmans, 2007).

Notes

[1] From *Charles Wesley: A Reader*, edited by John R. Tyson (Oxford University Press, 1989); page 59.

[2] From *A Plain Account of Christian Perfection*, by John Wesley (Beacon Hill Press of Kansas City, 1986); page 10.

[3] From *A Plain Account of Christian Perfection*; see http://gbgm-umc.org/UMhistory/Wesley/perfect1.html.

[4] From *A Plain Account of Christian Perfection*; page 11.

[5] From *John Wesley*, edited by Albert Outler (Oxford University Press, 1964); page 44.

[6] From *The Journal of Charles Wesley*; see http://wesley.nnu.edu/charles_wesley/journal/1738b.htm.

[7] From *The Journal of Charles Wesley*; see http://wesley.nnu.edu/charles_wesley/journal/1738b.htm.

[8] From *The Journal of John Wesley*; see http://www.godrules.net/library/wesley/274wesley_a6.htm.

[9] From *The Journal of Charles Wesley*, edited by Thomas Jackson (Baker Book House, 1980); I:159.

[10] From *Charles Wesley: A Reader*; page 103.

[11] From *Charles Wesley: A Reader*; pages 103–104.

[12] From *The Works of John Wesley*, edited by Thomas Jackson (The Wesleyan Conference Office, 1872); 14:320.

[13] From *The Works of John Wesley*; XIV:320–321.

[14] From *The Works of John Wesley*; VIII:270–271.

[15] From *The Works of John Wesley*; XIV:321.

[16] From *The Journal of Charles Wesley*, edited by Thomas Jackson; I:250.

[17] From *The Works of John Wesley*; VIII:279.

XII

Karl Barth
(1886–1968)

The Word of God

Has there ever been a time in your life when you wished you could hear directly from God? Perhaps you were facing a personal trial or vocational dilemma or you had an important decision to make. How wonderful it would have been to have God phone you so you could talk things over! Yes, there are times when we are desperate to hear from God. This is the situation in which Karl Barth found himself, and this is why his story is so relevant to our own.

* * * *

In the twilight years of the First World War, Karl Barth faced a spiritual crisis of the sort that comes upon many Christian people from time to time: a crisis of meaning. For Barth this crisis was all the more acute because as pastor of the Reformed Church in Safenwil, Switzerland, he had been entrusted with the care of souls and with the responsibility of preaching the Word of God.

Barth had been superbly educated and was a self-styled disciple of the famous church historian Adolf Harnack. He had studied with many of the leading intellectual lights of his day, including Wilhelm Hermann. Barth had entered the pastorate with his theology well intact. As he explained, "For twelve years I was a minister....I *had* my theology. It was not really mine, to be sure, but that of my unforgotten teacher Wilhelm Hermann, grafted upon the principles which I had learned, less consciously than unconsciously, in my native home."[1] Barth had been schooled in the ethical theology of his day, which stressed the universal fatherhood of God, the brotherhood of the human race, and the perfectibility of human nature. The carnage of World War I had begun to erode Barth's optimism about human nature, however; and soon he began to doubt whether the human race could resolve its own problems. In the face of global forces of evil and senseless violence, human life seemed increasingly cheap and meaningless.

As early as 1910, Karl Barth had begun to notice that fewer and fewer of the students who embraced the modern theology answered the call to pastoral service. His shrewd evaluation of this situation pointed to two flaws in the new approach. The first was a "religious individualism" that made all norms seem irrelevant, and the second was "historical relativism" which suggested that there were no historically based absolutes in Christian theology or ethics.[2] In 1911, Barth accepted the call to the pastorate in Safenwil; and his gradual slide into theological crisis continued unabated. As he reported, "Once in the ministry, I found myself growing away from those theological habits of thought [which he had formerly embraced] and being forced back at every point more and more upon the specific *minister*'s problem, *the sermon*. I sought to find my way between the problem of human life on the one hand and the content of the Bible on the other."[3] This location, between the problem of human life and the content of the Bible, caused Karl Barth to begin reading the Bible more closely; and he began to read the Bible differently.

Barth began to distinguish more clearly between *The Word of God and the Word of Man*, as the title of his publication of his early lectures (1928) described the situation. He had become convinced that the earlier theology went to the Bible with the wrong presuppositions and the wrong starting point, treating the Bible as a human word—human words *about* God, rather than words *from* God. Hence Barth subsequently reminded his readers that the Bible communicates the Word of God. As Barth declared,

> It is not the right human thoughts about God which form the content of the Bible, but the right divine thoughts about men. The Bible tells us not how we should talk with God but what he says to us; not how we find the way to him; but how he has sought and found the way to us; not the right relation in which we must place ourselves to him, but the covenant [relationship] which he has made with all who are Abraham's spiritual children and which he has sealed

once and for all in Jesus Christ. It is this which is within the Bible. The word of God is within the Bible.[4]

In his fresh reading of the Bible, Karl Barth met a God who speaks and calls to his people. The Bible could no longer be read like a history book of past events or a record of past revelation; it became instead a vehicle for present and future revelation. "Revelation" for Barth came to mean one should expect to have a "crisis," or a contemporary encounter with the living God through God's Word. This divine-human encounter is facilitated by the Bible because in the Bible we are confronted by the call of God.

In 1916, while war ravaged the world and Europe was searching for truth and meaning, Karl Barth was invited to give a lecture at the small Swiss town of Lentwil. The lecture he presented on that occasion showed the impact of his new way of reading the Bible; it was entitled "The Strange New World Within the Bible."[5]

Barth introduced his hearers to a God who speaks to us through the words of the Bible. "We are with Abraham in Haran. We hear a call which commands him: Get thee out of thy country, and from thy kindred, unto a land that I will show thee! We hear a promise: I will make of thee a great nation. And Abraham believed in the Lord; and he counted it to him for righteousness. What is the meaning of all this?"[6] Next Barth visited Moses in the wilderness: "Suddenly there comes to him also a call: Moses, Moses!—a great command: Come now therefore, and I will send thee unto Pharaoh, that thou mayest bring forth my people, the children of Israel, out of Egypt!—and a simple assurance: Certainly I will be with thee. Here again are words and experiences which seem at first to be nothing but riddles. We do not read the like either in the daily papers or in other books. What lies behind [it]?"[7]

After marching his hearers through the calls of Abraham, Moses, Gideon, and Elijah, Barth allowed them to stand in the presence of a Jesus "who was no prophet, no poet, no hero, no thinker, and yet all of these and more! His words cause alarm, for he speaks with authority and not as we ministers. With compelling power he calls to each one: Follow me! Even to the distrustful and antagonistic he gives an irresistible impression of 'eternal life.'"[8] In the words of the Bible we hear the call of God, the call of our Lord Jesus Christ; it is a call to faith and repentance. And where we are prone to try to interpret these words and wrestle meaning from them for ourselves, Barth suggested another route. Rather than first trying to interpret the Word, perhaps we should first allow the Word to interpret us and to interpret itself. Hence Barth urged,

> The Holy Scriptures will interpret themselves in spite of all our human limitations. We need only dare to follow this drive, this spirit, this river, to grow out beyond ourselves toward the highest answer. This daring is *faith*; and we read the Bible rightly, not when we do so with false modesty, restraint, and attempted sobriety, for these are passive qualities, but when we read it in faith. And the invitation to dare and to reach toward the highest, even though we do not deserve it, is the expression of *grace* in the Bible: the Bible unfolds to us as we are met, guided, drawn on, and made to grow by the grace of God.[9]

Thus, Barth described the Bible as "the history of God," which he contrasted with the history of humans: "We have found in the Bible a new world, God, God's sovereignty, God's glory, God's incomprehensible love. Not the history of man but the history of God!"[10] This realization causes a series of questions to break in on a person's mind: "Who then is God? What is his will? What are his thoughts? What is the mysterious 'other,' new greater world which emerges in the Bible beyond all the ways of men, summoning us to a decision to believe or not to believe? In Whom did Abraham believe?...In whose power did Christ die and rise again? Whose name did the Apostles proclaim? The contents of the Bible are 'God.' But what is the content of these contents?"[11] The inner truth of the Bible, which the Bible answers well enough, is that "God is the Lord and the Redeemer, the Saviour and Comforter of all the souls that turn to him; and the new world is the kingdom of blessedness."[12]

Karl Barth taught twentieth-century people to expect to hear the call of God in the Bible. He taught them to read the Bible in faith, in search of grace, hoping to learn more about God so that they might more accurately understand themselves and their problems. But more than mere answers, however truthful and profound these answers may be, the Bible, as the vehicle of God's Word, offers us a fresh encounter with the living God through Jesus Christ.

Karl Barth insisted that Christians serve a speaking God, that God continues to speak to God's people through his Word. On another occasion Barth wrote, "The Word of God is the Word that God *spoke, speaks*, and *will speak* in the midst of men. Regardless of whether it is heard or not, it is, in itself, directed to all men."[13]

God's Word and work among humans is the gospel, the good news of God's acceptance of sinful humans through faith in Jesus Christ. In the gospel Barth found both God's "Yes" and God's "No." The gospel is God's "Yes" to us; it is the message of God's acceptance and reconciling grace. But the gospel also includes God's "No" to human sin. This is the message of the cross of Jesus Christ; it is God saying "Yes" to fallen humans and simultaneously saying "No" to human sin. But because our God is a gracious God, his "No" is never separated from his "Yes." Indeed, his cross offers the path of repentance and faith that takes us through God's "No" to sin so that we might find God acceptance, God's "Yes" to us in Jesus Christ. Just as the gospel includes both a divine "Yes" and "No," so also it requires a decision of faith ("Yes") or disbelief ("No") on the part of humans.

In 1919, Karl Barth found himself drawn to Paul's Letter to the Romans. Barth's close study of the epistle was transformative for him, as it had been for Augustine, Martin Luther, and many others. In Romans, he met classical Christian doctrines, like revelation, sin, justification by faith, grace, and life in the Holy Spirit. Barth brought these doctrines into connection with his desire and design to listen to God's Word as he read the Bible. When Barth published his study *The Epistle to the Romans* in 1919, it was printed by a small publisher; only 1,000 copies were produced. But by 1922, Barth had completely revised the work from the standpoint of his new way of reading the Bible and his newfound appreciation for the Bible's main themes. It became a runaway bestseller!

Utterly surprised by this response, Karl Barth likened the reception of *The Epistle to the Romans* to a situation in which he had found himself in the country church at Pratteln. He came back to the church at night, and in the dark he lost his balance. Reaching out into the darkness to grasp something to break his fall, he inadvertently grabbed the bell rope! He rode it up and down several times, ringing out an unintentional alarm before he regained his feet.[14] Such was the surprising effect of the second edition of Karl Barth's *The Epistle to the Romans*!

As Barth gradually refurbished Christian doctrines, giving them a new and modern urgency, experts called his theology "Neo-Orthodoxy," which amounted to calling it "new-old classical truths," or "classical Christian truths affirmed in a new way." Karl Barth called his theology a "theology of crisis" because it was born in an intellectual and spiritual crisis in his own life and because he believed that the heart of Christian theology was a personal encounter with the living God through Jesus Christ—An encounter of this magnitude is a "crisis" indeed!

Over the course of his life, and the first half of the twentieth century, Karl Barth produced his famous *Church Dogmatics*. Like Aquinas' earlier *Summa Theologica*, Barth's *Dogmatics* was a work of monumental proportions. Unfinished, it spanned more than 9,000 pages in the original German edition. Barth's influence was even larger than his literary endeavors, however. He is generally considered a "modern church father"; and his combination of old theological verities with new, modern sensibilities left an enduring legacy among modern Christians, Protestants and Roman Catholics alike.

God continues to speak to his people through God's Word. As Barth explained, "We serve a speaking God." In God's Word, Jesus Christ, we hear God's resounding "Yes!" to us and a simultaneous "No!" to our sin. In the Bible, understood as the vehicle of God's Word, we can learn to hear God's voice. We can hear God's call to faith and obedience. In and through the stories of Abraham, Isaac, Jacob, Moses, Ruth, and Esther, Jesus and the apostles, God continues to speak to us about faithfulness and action, about what we should do and whom we should become. In his Word we are able to encounter a living God and hear his voice speak to us afresh today.

Prayer

Gracious God, I know that you do not leave your children in perpetual silence. Help me listen for your voice as I study your Word. Give me the courage to be faithful and obedient to what you call me to do, and help me become what you would have me to be. What a blessing it is to serve a speaking God! In the name of Jesus, the Word, I pray. **Amen.**

Questions for Reflection

1. When he had a personal theological crisis, Karl Barth turned to the Bible. Where do you turn when you feel doubt or confusion about the relevancy of your Christian faith?

2. How do you distinguish between the words of humans and the Word of God?

3. In what ways has Christianity been shaped (negatively) by modern intellectual forces like individualism and relativism?

4. Have you ever heard the voice of God call you to faith or to action while you were reading the Bible? If so, how did this experience affect you? How did it affect others?

5. When you read the Bible, do you look for information *about* God or do you anticipate an encounter *with* God? Or both? Why?

For Further Reading

Evangelical Theology, by Karl Barth (William B. Eerdmans Publishing Company, 1963).

Jesus Is Victor!, by Donald Bloesch (Abingdon Press, 1976).

Karl Barth, by David L. Muller (Word Books, 1972).

Notes

[1] From *The Word of God and the Word of Man*, by Karl Barth (Hodder and Stoughton, 1928); page 100.
[2] From *Karl Barth*, by David L. Mueller (Word Books, 1972); page 18.
[3] From *The Word of God and the Word of Man*; page 100.
[4] From *The Word of God and the Word of Man*; page 43.
[5] From *The Word of God and the Word of Man*; pages 28–50 contain the text of this address.
[6] From *The Word of God and the Word of Man*; page 28.
[7] From *The Word of God and the Word of Man*; page 29.
[8] From *The Word of God and the Word of Man*; page 30.
[9] From *The Word of God and the Word of Man*; page 34.

[10] From *The Word of God and the Word of Man*; page 45.

[11] From *The Word of God and the Word of Man*; pages 45–46.

[12] From *The Word of God and the Word of Man*; page 46.

[13] From *Evangelical Theology*, by Karl Barth (William B. Eerdmans Publishing Company, 1963); page 18.

[14] From *Karl Barth: His Life From Letters and Autobiographical Texts*, by Eberhard Busch (Fortress Press, 1975); pages 120–121.

XIII

Dietrich Bonhoeffer
(1906–1945)

The Cost of Discipleship

Some people look on Christianity as a set of ideas or doctrines. Other people view Christianity as a lifestyle and a collection of practices. Dietrich Bonhoeffer, because of very challenging circumstances in his own life, came to see Christianity as a matter of personal discipleship. He viewed it as a personal adherence to and following of the living Christ. Like the disciples of old who heard the call of Jesus ("Follow me") as they mended their nets on the shores of the Sea of Galilee, Bonhoeffer urged modern Christians to understand themselves not simply as believers in a tradition or as practitioners of a certain way of life, but rather as followers of the living Lord.

Bonhoeffer's story is challenging to us because it reminds us of the costly nature of true discipleship and the hard choices that a person may have to face when he or she decides to follow Jesus in an uncompromising way.

* * * *

The German Lutheran pastor and author Dietrich Bonhoeffer stared out the narrow window of his cell in Flossenburg prison as rain pelted down on the dismal landscape. It was 1945, and he had been in prison for over two years. What was his crime? Trying to be faithful to the gospel of Jesus Christ in the midst of an oppressive political regime.

From 1930–1936, Bonhoeffer had been a notable professor at the University of Berlin. As Germany gradually came under the grip of Adolf Hitler and the Nazi party, Dietrich Bonhoeffer, along with Karl Barth and others, drafted a theological declaration that urged German Christians to stand apart from the state church because it was supporting Nazism. Completed in 1934, the Barmen Declaration signaled the creation of the "Confessing Church" in Germany. This church refused to cooperate with the Nazis and condemned the state church for its complicity in the government's political agenda. The Barmen Declaration's posture of opposition placed its authors in grave danger.

In 1935, as the official German Lutheran seminaries fell in line behind Nazi ideology, Bonhoeffer founded a seminary for the Confessing Church in the village of Finkenwalde. Its rural location gave him the opportunity to train ministers who were able to question freely the direction of German politics. Many of these students and their professors would soon be imprisoned for refusing induction into the German army. In 1937, the seminary was closed by the Nazis; and Bonhoeffer gradually drifted from the public eye. He lived in seclusion, teaching, writing, and operating an "underground" seminary for another three years.

In 1937, Bonhoeffer wrote one of his first theological treatises. It was entitled *The Cost of Discipleship*, and in it he explored the pressing question of what it means to be a Christian in difficult times—times such as his own. In this study Dietrich distinguished sharply between what he termed "cheap grace" and "costly grace."

"Cheap grace is the deadly enemy of our Church," he wrote.[1] "Cheap grace," he continued, "means grace sold on the market like cheapjacks' wares. The sacraments, the forgiveness of sin, and the consolations of religion are thrown away at cut prices. Grace is presented as the Church's inexhaustible treasury, from which she showers blessings with generous hands, without asking questions or fixing limits. Grace without price; grace without cost!"[2] "Cheap grace" was what the German state church conferred on people who saw no inconsistency between what they were doing as Nazis and the call of Jesus Christ. Hence Bonhoeffer wrote, "Cheap grace means the justification of sin without the justification of the sinner."[3] People were being forgiven, but they were not being challenged to change or to turn from their wrongdoing.

Bonhoeffer explained the way in which "cheap grace" undermined the true gospel of Jesus Christ by examining how "cheap grace" is manifested in the Church: "Cheap grace is the preaching of forgiveness without requiring repentance, baptism without church discipline, Communion without confession, absolution without personal confession. Cheap grace is grace without discipleship, grace without the cross, grace without Jesus Christ, living and incarnate."[4] Hence he concluded, "Cheap grace is the grace we bestow on ourselves."[5]

The opposite of this counterfeit grace is "costly grace." It is the true grace of the gospel of Jesus Christ. "Costly grace" is a call to forgiveness and discipleship to the living Christ. As Bonhoeffer wrote, "Costly grace is the treasure hidden in the field; for the sake of it a man will gladly go and sell all that he has. It is the pearl of great price to buy which the merchant will sell all his goods. It is the kingly rule of Christ, for whose sake a man will pluck out the eye which causes him to stumble, it is the call of Jesus Christ at which the disciple leaves his nets and follows him."[6]

Whereas "cheap grace" turns God's grace into a bandage to cover our sins, "costly grace" stresses that forgiveness results in a transformation of a person's life through a living relationship with the living Jesus Christ. Bonhoeffer explained in what sense true grace is "costly":

> Such grace is *costly* because it calls us to follow and it is *grace* because it calls us to follow *Jesus Christ*. It is costly because it costs a man his life, and it is grace because it gives a man the only true life. It is costly because it condemns sin, and grace because it justifies the sinner. Above all, it is *costly* because it costs God the life of his Son: "ye were bought with a price," and what has cost God much cannot be cheap for us. Above all, it is *grace* because God did not reckon his Son too dear a price to pay for our life, but delivered him up for us.[7]

For Bonhoeffer, "costly grace" confronts us with the call to follow Jesus; and it costs a person the surrender of her or his life. "Grace is costly," he wrote, "because it compels a man to submit to the yoke of Christ and follow him; it is grace because Jesus says: 'My yoke is easy and my burden is light.'"[8]

Costly grace is the call to Christian discipleship. It is a call to a living relationship with the living Jesus Christ. This is not adherence to a system of doctrine; it is a call to personal obedience. Faith is implicit in obeying the call to follow Jesus. "The call goes forth, and is at once followed by the response of obedience. The response of the disciples is an act of obedience, not a confession of faith in Jesus."[9]

The concept of discipleship, for Bonhoeffer, lays bare the true meaning of Christianity. "When we are called to follow Christ," he wrote, "we are summoned to an exclusive attachment to his person. The grace of his call bursts all the bonds of legalism. It is a gracious call, a gracious commandment. It transcends the difference between the law and the gospel. Christ calls, the disciple follows: that is grace and commandment in one. 'I will walk at liberty, for I seek thy commandments' (Ps. 119:45)."[10]

Discipleship means concrete, personal adherence to Jesus Christ. As Bonhoeffer explained,

> Discipleship means adherence to Christ, and, because Christ is the object of that adherence, it must take the form of discipleship. An abstract Christology, a doctrinal system, a general religious knowledge on the subject of grace or on the forgiveness of sins, render discipleship superfluous, and in fact they positively exclude any idea of discipleship whatever, and are essentially inimical to the whole conception of following Christ. With an abstract idea it is possible to enter into a relation of formal knowledge, to become enthusiastic about it, and perhaps even to put it into practice; but it can never be followed in personal obedience. Christianity without the living Christ is inevitably Christianity without discipleship, and Christianity without discipleship is always Christianity without Christ.[11]

The way of discipleship is a living relationship with the living Christ. It is a way of self-denial. Here the call to discipleship merges with the message of the cross. "'If any man would come after me,' [Jesus said] 'let him deny himself.'...Self-denial is never just a series of isolated acts of mortification or asceticism. It is not suicide, for there is an element of self-will even in that. To deny oneself is to be aware only of Christ and no more of self, to see only him who goes before [us] and no more the road which is too hard for us. Once more, all that self-denial can say is: 'He leads the way, keep close to Him.'"[12]

For Christ and for Christians the way of the cross is a way of suffering. Bonhoeffer wrote, "The cross is there, right from the beginning, he [the Christian] has only got to pick it up; there is no need for him deliberately to run after suffering. Jesus says that every Christian has his own cross waiting for him, a cross destined and appointed by God."[13]

The first cross that Christ lays on all Christians is experiencing the call to abandon the attachments of this world and surrender our lives to Christ. As Bonhoeffer wrote,

> As we embark on discipleship we surrender ourselves to Christ in union with his death—we give over our lives to death. Thus it begins; the cross is not the

terrible end to an otherwise god-fearing and happy life, but it meets us at the beginning of our communion with Christ. When Christ calls a man, he bids him come and die. It may be a death like that of the first disciples who had to leave home and work to follow him, or it may be a death like Luther's, who had to leave the monastery and go out into the world. But it is the same death every time—death in Jesus Christ, the death of the old man at his call.[14]

The way of discipleship, because of the cross, is invariably a way of suffering. "Suffering, then, is the badge of true discipleship,"[15] Bonhoeffer wrote. A disciple is not above his or her Master. "If we refuse to take up our cross and submit to suffering and rejection at the hands of men, we forfeit our fellowship with Christ and have ceased to follow him. But if we lose our lives in his service and carry our cross, we shall find our lives again in the fellowship of the cross with Christ."[16] Thus Bonhoeffer concluded, "Discipleship means allegiance to the suffering Christ, and it is therefore not at all surprising that Christians should be called upon to suffer."[17]

In 1939, Dietrich Bonhoeffer was invited to join the faculty of Union Theological Seminary in New York City. He accepted the post—perhaps out of frustration at his inability to change the situation in Germany—and arrived in New York on June 12, 1939. But by July 25 he was back in Germany; he could not live and teach in safety while so many he had taught and encouraged continued to live and work in peril.

As the war broke out, Bonhoeffer escaped direct service in the military by acting as a courier for German Military Intelligence; and in this service he was able to travel in Germany without interference from the Gestapo. He continued to teach and preach secretly as he traveled.

During this time, members of Military Intelligence, including the head of the department, began to oppose Hitler's rule in Germany. With the closing of the seminary in Finkenwalde, Bonhoeffer had gradually joined his brother-in-law and several high ranking generals in Hitler's cabinet in a plot to assassinate *Der Führer*. With an official governmental pass in his pocket, Bonhoeffer traveled throughout Germany and across Europe—working for the resistance. His role in the plot against Hitler was to use his contacts and speaking engagements to rally support for the overthrow of Hitler and to bring friendly governments to the assistance of the resistance.

A Christian pacifist, Bonhoeffer struggled with the question of involvement in the assassination plot. In the end, he likened it to a situation in which a madman had taken control of a city bus, weaving here and there through traffic and surging over the sidewalks, running over pedestrians and vehicles and causing massive destruction and injury. What should fellow passengers do? Should they sit by and allow the destruction to continue? Or should they try to wrestle the lunatic's hands from the steering wheel? Bonhoeffer viewed his involvement in the resistance not so much as an act of heroism, but as a duty. He viewed it as the lesser of two evils as he resolved to help take "the steering wheel" out of Hitler's hands. As Bonhoeffer used to say, "It is not only my task to look after the victims of madmen who drive a motorcar in a crowded street, but to do all in my power to stop their driving at all."[18]

After two separate attempts against Hitler's life had failed, the conspiracy was discovered; and the paper trail led to Dietrich Bonhoeffer (along with many others). In 1943 he was imprisoned for committing treason, opposing the draft, and refusing military service. He was tortured and interrogated by the Gestapo. While Bonhoeffer was in prison, a third unsuccessful attempt was made on Hitler's life; and once again Bonhoeffer was implicated (through his connections at Military Intelligence). Once again he was tortured and interrogated; Hitler wanted to capture and kill all the conspirators.

As the Second World War ground to a close, Bonhoeffer and his fellow political prisoners were moved from prison to prison in order to prevent their liberation by Allied troops. After almost two years in prison, Dietrich Bonhoeffer was hanged in Flossenburg prison camp, just one month prior to the end of the war and the liberation of Germany. He did indeed pay the cost of Christian discipleship.

We may not be called on to stand against an anti-Christian political regime. And we may not be called on to try to decide whether or not it is appropriate for us to help bring down an oppressive and destructive government. But Bonhoeffer's call to consider Christianity to be discipleship—nothing more or less than following the living Christ—speaks powerfully to our own times. Too often we find ourselves taking shortcuts in our life of faith. We want forgiveness, but we really do not want to have to change. Too often we find ourselves making compromises that we know Jesus Christ would never make and would not condone. Bonhoeffer's call to costly discipleship cuts across all conventions and across all compromises to challenge us afresh with the utter and radical simplicity of Jesus' demands on our lives.

Prayer

My Lord Jesus Christ, give me the courage to follow you with my whole heart and my whole self. Like Bonhoeffer, help me disdain compromises that dishonor you and cheapen my faith. Help me leave my "nets" behind and walk boldly with you into a new future. In your name I pray. **Amen.**

Questions for Reflection

1. Do you think of your Christian faith as a life of discipleship with Jesus Christ? Why or why not?

2. Do you see "cheap grace" at work in your own life or church? If so, how?

3. How do you understand "costly grace"? How does it shape your life as a Christian?

4. Do you agree with Bonhoeffer that "costly grace" leads to genuine Christian discipleship? Why or why not? How is this different from an intellectual faith or a hypothetical faith?

5. Bonhoeffer insisted that true discipleship invariably leads to suffering; it certainly did for him. What do you think about this assertion? Has your discipleship ever brought suffering into your life? How might this occur?

For Further Reading

The Cost of Discipleship, by Dietrich Bonhoeffer (Macmillan Publishing Co., Inc., 1977).

Letters and Papers From Prison, by Dietrich Bonhoeffer (Macmillan, 1962).

Dietrich Bonhoeffer: A Biography, by Eberard Bethge and Victoria J. Barrett (Augsburg Fortress, 2000).

Notes

[1] From *The Cost of Discipleship*, by Dietrich Bonhoeffer (Macmillan Publishing Co., Inc., 1977); page 45.

[2] From *The Cost of Discipleship*; page 45.

[3] From *The Cost of Discipleship*; page 46.

[4] From *The Cost of Discipleship*; page 47.

[5] From *The Cost of Discipleship*; page 47.

[6] From *The Cost of Discipleship*; page 47.

[7] From *The Cost of Discipleship*; pages 47–48.

[8] From *The Cost of Discipleship*; page 48.

[9] From *The Cost of Discipleship*; page 61.

[10] From *The Cost of Discipleship*; page 63.

[11] From *The Cost of Discipleship*; pages 63–64.

[12] From *The Cost of Discipleship*; page 97.

[13] From *The Cost of Discipleship*; page 98.

[14] From *The Cost of Discipleship*; page 99.

[15] From *The Cost of Discipleship*; page 100.

[16] From *The Cost of Discipleship*; page 101.

[17] From *The Cost of Discipleship*; page 101.

[18] From *The Cost of Discipleship*; page 28.

XIV

Martin Luther King, Jr.
(1929–1968)

Love Your Enemies

It is not difficult to find enmity and opposition in the contemporary world and social climate. Some people are willing to hate and oppose us simply because of who we are or what we believe. How easy it is to respond to opposition with enmity or to respond to hate with hate! Yet someone has to stop the cycle of hate and enmity before it escalates into violence. Someone has to point us to a better way. This is where the witness of Dr. Martin Luther King, Jr., speaks to us. He rightly recognized that "Love your enemies" was Jesus' most-difficult command to follow. Nevertheless, in the midst of a culture charged with racial hatred, Dr. King insisted that contemporary Christians must follow Jesus' difficult demand because there was no other reasonable solution to the growing cycle of hate and violence that was consuming our land.

* * * *

Born and reared in Atlanta, Georgia, Martin Luther King, Jr., was the son and grandson of Baptist ministers. While he was a student at Morehouse College (B.A., 1948), he too responded to the call to ministerial service. He studied for the ministry at Crozer Theological Seminary (B.D., 1951) and earned the Ph.D. degree in Systematic Theology at Boston University (1955). He later recalled that the first twenty-four years of his life were satisfying and were not plagued with problems. He had parents who loved him and who provided for him throughout the years of his formal education. His real trials began when he assumed leadership of the Montgomery bus boycott.[1]

In 1954, Dr. King became pastor of Dexter Avenue Baptist Church in Montgomery, Alabama. A year later, he was catapulted into notoriety when he became president of the Montgomery Improvement Association and leader of the Montgomery bus boycott. The boycott was organized to protest segregationist policies on city public transportation. When Rosa Parks refused to surrender her seat on a bus to a white person, these segregationist policies were brought to national attention. African American citizens of Montgomery boycotted public transportation until the official policies that perpetuated racial discrimination and segregation were overturned.

As president of the Montgomery Improvement Association, Dr. King was at the forefront of this campaign. During the Montgomery boycott he further developed his nonviolent approach to social change, and in this approach he believed he was following the principles of Jesus. He had also studied the nonviolent approach to social change that Gandhi had pioneered in India.

In a sermon Dr. King reported that threatening phone calls and letters started coming to his home when the protest began. As they increased in their number and severity, he realized that the threats were real. After one particularly upsetting call, he wrote that his fears overwhelmed him and brought him to a point of saturation.[2] After pacing the floor for what seemed to be hours, Dr. King realized that he could not return to sleep; so he went down to the kitchen and made a pot of coffee. His resolve was deeply shaken as he worried about his family, his personal safety, and the lives of those he loved. When he felt he was ready to give up, he turned to God in prayer.

Dr. King turned his kitchen table into an altar as he prayed out loud that he was afraid; that he knew if he did not demonstrate courageous leadership, the people would falter; and that he could not face this task alone.[3] At that moment, Dr. King experienced God's presence in a way that was both extremely precious and calming. He felt that he heard an inner voice telling him to stand up for righteousness and truth because God was with him. Dr. King's fear and uncertainty melted away. He felt that he could face whatever happened.

Nothing had changed in terms of the circumstances Dr. King was facing, but now he met them with a new sense of peace.[4] True to the dire words of the telephone threat, Dr. King's home was bombed three nights later. Providentially, no one was harmed. In spite of the bombing, Dr. King remained undeterred in his struggle to bring racial justice to his people and parish. His experience of God's presence had become for him a source of strength and trust. He knew that God would continue to give him the inner resources he needed to face all the storms and challenges of his demanding life.[5]

Dr. King based his philosophy of nonviolent social change on the teachings of Jesus. In a sermon entitled "Loving Your Enemies," he called attention to the words of Jesus Christ, "Ye have heard that it hath been said, Thou shalt love thy neighbor, and hate thine enemy. But I say unto you, Love your enemies, bless them that curse you, do good to them that hate you, and pray for them that despitefully use you, and persecute you; that ye may be the children of your Father which is in heaven" (Matthew 5:43-45, KJV). Dr. King acknowledged that this command is probably the most difficult of Jesus' teachings to follow.[6] Yet throughout the balance of the sermon, he insisted that Jesus' words are both practical and necessary; indeed, given the level of hate and violence in our modern world, Jesus' words come to us with a new urgency because they hold within them the potential for breaking the cycle of violence that has become so much a part of modern life. As Dr. King summarized, Jesus was not naive about the difficulty of heeding this admonition. Indeed, it is only out of an absolute and total surrender of self to God that loving our enemies becomes possible. Dr. King reminded his hearers of the absolute urgency of following this teaching. He considered it to be a primary Christian responsibility to live out this injunction each and every day.[7]

As he inquired about how we can love our enemies, Dr. King stressed the importance of developing and maintaining a capacity to forgive. He believed that it is not possible to love one's enemies unless one is willing to forgive them.[8] He rightly concluded that the forgiving act must begin with those who have been wronged. It is within their power alone to forgive. But forgiveness does not mean ignoring an evil or placing a false label on an evil act as if we were somehow calling it "good." Forgiveness simply refuses to allow the evil to be a barrier to relationship with that person. Dr. King taught that real forgiveness does not mean that we will forgive someone but we will not forget what this person did. Nor does genuine forgiveness mean that we will forgive someone but we will not have anything to do with this person because of what she or he did. Contrary to these attitudes, forgiveness means the willingness to reconcile.[9] Loving our enemies becomes more possible if we recognize that the evil deed that our fellow human being has done to us—the thing that hurts us—is not the sum total of the enemy's person or character. Dr. King believed that both good and evil reside in every human being. The evil that resides in people never represents all that they are. No one is completely evil, and no one is beyond the reach of God's redemptive love.[10]

Dr. King also reminds us that we love our enemies by taking practical steps to win their friendship and understanding. We do not strive to humiliate or defeat them. Our goal is to win their friendship, not to bring about their downfall. This kind of love is much deeper and more demanding than mere emotion or sentimentalism. It is rather the *agape* love, the other-directed, selfless love with which God loves people. This is the love described in John 3:16: "For God so loved the world that he gave his only Son, so that everyone who believes in him may not perish but may have eternal life." This is an other-directed love that longs for the best for the other person. It is also a love that takes redemptive action. It gives, sends, forgives, and reconciles. Therefore, Dr. King concluded that when Jesus calls us to love our enemies, he is calling us to have this same *agape* love and in so doing, become children of God.[11]

When exploring the theoretical dimension of the admonition to love our enemies, Dr. King was equally practical. His first reason for loving our enemies was that only love has the power to break the chain of evil and conflict. To return hate for hate simply perpetuates and increases the hatred.[12]

The second reason is that hate harms the person who hates much more than it harms the person at whom the hate is directed. Dr. King rightly asserted that it harms the essential and vital unity of the personality. In stark contrast, love is the power that unites the personality and makes it whole.[13]

The third reason for loving our enemies is that love is the only force that is capable of turning our enemy into our friend. Dr. King pointed out that meeting hate with hate will not get rid of the enemy. It is by getting rid of enmity that we have the possibility of turning an enemy into a friend. Love has transforming power.[14]

The final and most-explicit reason we should love our enemies comes to us directly from Jesus' teaching: "that you may be children of your Father in heaven" (Matthew 5:45). We are to love our enemies for the simple reason that God, through our Lord Jesus Christ, has told us to do so. God has called us to this difficult task as a portion of our lot in being God's children. Yet it is precisely our being children of God that makes loving our enemies both possible and desirable for us. Love, particularly love toward our enemies, makes it possible for us to know God and to experience God's holiness.[15]

From the Montgomery bus boycott, Dr. King went on to found the Southern Christian Leadership Conference, which addressed civil rights issues and racial prejudice across the country. In 1963, he led the "March on Washington" to highlight issues of poverty and racial equality. During this event he delivered his famous "I Have a Dream Speech" from the steps of the Lincoln Memorial. In 1964, Dr. King was awarded the Noble Peace Price (He was the youngest man ever to receive it.) for his tireless efforts at nonviolent social change.

Martin Luther King, Jr., was assassinated on April 4, 1968, in Memphis, Tennessee, while assisting the city's garbage workers in their strike against unfair wages and discriminatory hiring practices.

To some people it might seem that Dr. King's approach to Christian, nonviolent social change was a failure because it resulted in his death. But Dr. King would have not seen it that way. He probably would have said that he was being faithful to what God called him to do. He was clearly being obedient to that most-difficult command of Jesus Christ, "Love your enemies." In maintaining his reformatory course and proclaiming his Christian values, Dr. King was able to raise the conscience of America and rally people of good faith to social causes that had long begged for redress. In this he certainly must be counted among the peacemakers Jesus described in Matthew 5:9 and who "will be called children of God." Fulfilling Dr. King's call to practice nonviolence and display Christian love—shown even toward one's enemies—remains as challenging on a personal and societal level as it was when he first issued it. We can be thankful that the transforming power of Christian love has not changed. Our troubled relationships and our violent world are as much in need of this witness as they were more than four decades ago.

Prayer

Lord, it troubles me to think that I have enemies; but I know I do. Either because of what I have said or what I have done or simply because of who I am, there are people who feel and express hostility toward me. I am sorry if I have been the cause of this hostility, and I repent of actions and words that might have contributed to it. I ask you to bless those who oppose me so that their hate might be turned into something more productive. I ask you to help me love my enemies and not harbor animosity toward those who oppose me. I thank you for Dr. King's insight about the destructive power of hate and the healing power of Christian love. Help me be counted among the peacemakers so that I too might be called a child of God. In the name of Jesus Christ, the Lamb of God, I pray. **Amen.**

Questions for Reflection

1. When Dr. King reached his "saturation point," filled with fear and uncertainty he turned to God and poured out his feelings in prayer. Where do you turn when you feel so weighed down that you cannot go on? Why?

2. Has God ever given you a sense of calm or assurance in response to your heartfelt prayer? If so, what were the circumstances?

3. Do Jesus' words, "Love your enemies" sound impractical to you? Why or why not?

4. How did Dr. King think we *could* love our enemies?

5. Why did Dr. King think we *should* love our enemies?

For Further Reading

Strength to Love, by Martin Luther King, Jr. (Fortress Press, 1963).

Stride Toward Freedom, by Martin Luther King, Jr. (Harper and Row, 1964).

The Autobiography of Martin Luther King, Jr., by Martin Luther King, Jr., with Clayborne Carson (Warner Books, 2001).

Notes

[1] See *Strength to Love*, by Martin Luther King, Jr. (Fortress Press, 1963); page 113.
[2] See *Strength to Love*; page 113.
[3] See *Strength to Love*; page 114.
[4] See *Strength to Love*; page 114.
[5] See *Strength to Love*; page 114.
[6] See *Strength to Love*; page 49.
[7] See *Strength to Love*; page 50.
[8] See *Strength to Love*; page 50.
[9] See *Strength to Love*; pages 50–51.
[10] See *Strength to Love*; page 51.
[11] See *Strength to Love*; pages 51–52.
[12] See *Strength to Love*; pages 52–53.
[13] See *Strength to Love*; page 53.
[14] See *Strength to Love*; page 54.
[15] See *Strength to Love*; page 55.

XV

Mother Teresa of Calcutta
(1910–1997)

Coworkers With Christ

W hat a privilege it is to be able to do deeds of Christian service! Great or small, these good works contribute to the betterment of humankind and the growth of the kingdom of God. Mother Teresa of Calcutta epitomizes selfless Christian service in our own times. She urged contemporary Christians to see themselves as "coworkers with Christ." It is not so much that we serve by doing things for Christ; in reality, when we serve others as a venue of Christian discipleship, we are— as Mother Teresa suggested—serving with Christ as his coworkers. On this basis, then, one would expect that as coworkers with Christ, we would always experience a powerful and sustained sense of Christ's presence through our service; but Mother Teresa's remarkable witness is that such is not always the case.

* * * *

It was a cold and blustery December day in Oslo, Norway. A small, frail-looking woman, who used to be known as Agnes Bojaxhiu, was clad only in her white Indian sari with blue border and sandals. She was about to receive the Nobel Peace Prize for her work in establishing the Missionaries of Charity. She had begun the movement in 1948 because of a persistent nudging from Jesus in her soul. Through her efforts the Missionaries of Charity became a worldwide Christian service organization that specialized in bringing the love of Christ to the poor and outcasts of society. But as she was being honored with the most-prestigious award the world has to offer, Mother Teresa's attention was riveted on the poor and the hungry: "[Jesus] makes himself the hungry one, the naked one, the homeless one, the sick one, the one in prison, the lonely one, the unwanted one, and he says: 'You did it to me.' He is hungry for our love, and this is the hunger of our poor people. This is the hunger that you and I must find, it may be in our own home."[1]

Mother had traveled the world over several times; and she was appalled at the pain and suffering in which people lived, even in the West. She used the occasion of her acceptance speech—given during the season of peace and goodwill to humankind—to draw attention to the suffering that has descended on the modern world. In addition to hunger and poverty, she attacked drug use and abortion. She viewed them as persistent problems that break God's peace in people's lives. Mother Teresa remarked painfully, "I was surprised in the West to see so many young boys and girls given into drugs, and I tried to find out why. . . . 'Because there is no one in the family to receive them.' Father and mother are so busy they have no time. . . . The child goes back to the street and gets involved in something. . . . These are things that break peace."[2] Mother Teresa painfully paralleled the destruction caused by abortion with the plague of infant mortality in India and Africa. She concluded, "Let us ensure this year that we make every single child born, and unborn, wanted. . . . Have we really made the children unwanted?"[3]

Ever since 1928, when she left her home as an eighteen-year-old young woman, she had been committed to serving Christ through service to the poor. After training at the Institute of the Blessed Virgin, in Ireland, she applied for missionary work in Bengal, India. She had first felt the call of God on her life at the tender age of twelve. She wrote,

> I was only twelve years old then. It was then I first knew I had a vocation to the poor, in 1922. I wanted to be a missionary, I wanted to go out and give the life of Christ to the people in the missionary countries. At the beginning, between twelve and eighteen I didn't want to become a nun. We were a happy family. But when I was eighteen, I decided to leave my home and become a nun, and since then, this forty years, I've never doubted even for a second that I've done the right thing; it was the will of God. It was His choice.[4]

After several years of spiritual and vocational training, Agnes Bojaxhiu became a Loreto nun named Sister Teresa. She remembered, "From the age of 5 ½ years,—when I first received Him [Jesus]—the love for souls has been within [me]—It grew with the years—until I came to India—with the hope of saving many souls."[5] A poem she penned at this time shows that she felt simultaneously the tug of her happy home in Skopje and the call of Christ on her life. But she moved confidently ahead, as she wrote, "My heart draws me onward / To serve my Christ."[6]

Serving in India, first as a teacher and then as a nurse, Sister Teresa saw tremendous suffering; and the alleviation of suffering became the focal point of her life and ministry. She wrote, "Suffering is increasing in the world today. People are hungry for something more beautiful, for something greater than people around about can give. There is a great hunger for God in the world today. Everywhere there is much suffering, but there is also great hunger for God and love for each other. There is hunger for ordinary bread, and there is hunger for love, for kindness, for thoughtfulness; and this is the greatest poverty that makes people suffer so much."[7]

After striving for eighteen years to bring the love and kindness of Christ to the people of India through her work as a Loreto nun, Sister Teresa had a dramatic encounter with Jesus Christ that would ultimately change the direction of her ministry. This encounter took place in September 1946. Mother Teresa would subsequently call it her "call within the call." It amounted to the inspiration for a new kind of ministry to the poor in which the missionaries lived directly among those they served and shared their lot in life in order to bring them the joy of Jesus Christ. She described the event as occurring during a train ride to her annual fall retreat: "[It] was a call within my vocation. It was a second calling. It was a vocation to give up even Loreto where I was very happy and to go out in the streets to serve the poorest of the poor. It was in that train, I heard the call to give up all and follow Him into the slums—to serve Him in the poorest of the poor. . . . I knew it was His will and that I had to follow Him. There was no doubt that it was going to be His work."[8]

The Missionaries of Charity, a religious order who lived and worked among the poor, would be the result of Sister Teresa's inspiration. After several arduous years of spiritual discernment and soul searching, she was finally given permission to leave her work at Loreto and establish the new order. This was a very significant pilgrimage for her because she had within her a powerful push—which she understood to be from the Lord—to begin to work on this new vocation immediately, while at the same time she was required to go through a corresponding external process of spiritual discernment whereby her ecclesiastical superiors could be convinced that it was the Lord's will that she start this work. For several years she seemed to be caught between an internal voice that urged her to hurry up and move ahead and external warnings from ecclesiastical superiors who told her to take her time, go slow, and wait. Finally, by the end of 1952, her new order had come to fruition and was operating in Calcutta. It was as founder and head of the Missionaries of Charity that Sister Teresa became "Mother Teresa."

Ironically, at precisely the time when Mother Teresa's inspiration and dream for Christian service was finally coming to fruition, a terrible silence descended on her soul. She had long been accustomed to a profound sense of the presence and direction of Christ, but beginning in 1949–50 there was nothing but silence. This silence led her to experience a sense of darkness and a feeling of abandonment by God. After years of bearing this feeling in silence, Mother Teresa began to discuss it privately (often by mail) with her spiritual director. At one point she avoided communicating with him because "she felt like an 'ice block'"[9] and did not want to waste his time. On other occasions, she unburdened herself at length:

> Now Father—since 49 or 50 this terrible sense of loss—this untold darkness—this loneliness [,] this continual longing for God—which gives me that pain deep down in my heart—Darkness is such that I really do not see—neither with my mind nor with my reason—the place of God in my soul is blank—There is no God in me—when the pain of longing is so great—I just long & long for God—then it is that I feel—He does not want me—He is not there—… God does not want me—Sometimes—I just hear my own heart cry out—"My God" and nothing else comes—The torture and pain I can't explain.[10]

What suffering this silence caused Mother Teresa! She had become accustomed to hearing the voice of Jesus Christ in her soul and feeling the direction of God in her life. Now she heard and felt nothing. This silence sometimes caused her to doubt herself and her ability to carry out the missionary work Christ had given her to do. Obviously, one answer to the dilemma was that she (and we) should not rely too heavily on feelings. Our acceptance before God does not depend on our *feeling* accepted by God. God's approval of us or our efforts does not always spell itself out in an inner sense of approval. As Mother Teresa's spiritual director, Archbishop Perier, told her,

God guides you, Dear Mother; you are not so much in the dark as you think. The path to be followed may not always be clear at once. Pray for light; do not decide too quickly, listen to what others have to say, consider their reasons. You will always find something to help you. You have exterior facts enough to see that God blesses your work. Therefore He is satisfied. Guided by faith by prayer and by reason with a right intention you have enough. Feelings are not required and often may be misleading.[11]

In the context of this dreadful inner silence, Mother Teresa learned to live completely by faith. As she wrote to a friend and confidant, "Pray for me—for within me everything is icy cold—It is only that blind faith that carries me through for in reality to me all is darkness. As long as Our Lord has all the pleasure—I really do not count."[12]

Mother Teresa had long been accustomed to sharing in the physical sufferings of Christ among the poor and the outcasts. It was in this sense that she and her Missionaries of Charity became "coworkers with Christ." She saw suffering as a part of Jesus' ministry, as well as of her own. "Suffering in itself," she wrote, "is nothing; but suffering shared with Christ's passion is a wonderful gift. Man's most beautiful gift is that he can share in the passion of Christ. Yes, a gift and a sign of his love; because this is how his Father proved that he loved the world—by giving his Son to die for us."[13] Or again she wrote, "Without our suffering, our work would just be social work, very good and helpful, but not the work of Jesus Christ, not part of the Redemption. Jesus wanted to help by sharing our life, our loneliness, our agony, our death. Only by being one with us has he redeemed us."[14]

In this way, then, Mother Teresa came to see her work among the poor as not only sharing in their suffering but also as sharing in Jesus' suffering among them. This was how the Missionaries of Charity became coworkers with Christ:

> As each Sister is to become a Co-Worker of Christ in the slums, each ought to understand what God and the Missionaries of Charity expect from her. Let Christ radiate and live his life in her and through her in the slums. Let the poor, seeing her, be drawn to Christ and invite him to enter their homes and their lives. Let the sick and suffering find in her a real angel of comfort and consolation. Let the little ones of the streets cling to her because she reminds them of him, the friend of the little ones.[15]

This same pattern of sharing in the sufferings of Christ supplied the insight Mother Teresa needed to help make sense of her desolate inner state. She subsequently wrote, "I have come to love the darkness."[16] As Father Brian Kolodiejchuk explained, "Mother Teresa's understanding of her inner condition deepened considerably; she came to realize that her darkness was the spiritual side of her work, a sharing in Christ's redemptive suffering."[17] Seeing her own spiritual pain as a part of the pain that Jesus Christ feels for the whole world caused Mother Teresa to find hope and joy in her spiritual struggles, even as she found hope and joy amidst the sufferings of the poor and outcasts. Just as Easter was the joy-filled culmination of Jesus' sufferings, so also the triumph over suffering will come to pass through Resurrection hope and faith. As she wrote, "The joy of loving Jesus comes from the joy of sharing in His sufferings. So do not allow yourself to be troubled or distressed, but believe in the joy of the Resurrection. In all our lives, as in the life of Jesus, the Resurrection has to come, the joy of Easter has to dawn."[18]

Someone has written to the effect that the next best thing to feeling God's presence is sensing God's absence. This is a remarkable thought which casts a modicum of light on Mother Teresa's spiritual insight. Feeling God's presence in our lives is a remarkable spiritual blessing, and we wish that it were always so. That is, we wish that the strong, palpable, guiding presence of God was always on us. Sometimes it is! And these moments and occasions stand out in our faith pilgrimage and memory as "mountain top" experiences. By their preciousness these kinds of experiences challenge and contradict the more-normal ones, in which we sense or feel almost nothing at all. The sense of the utter nearness of God teaches us what the absence of God feels like.

Without those experiences of nearness, we would not know when we were living through an experience of God's absence. Seen in the context of moments of God's precious nearness, these times of feeling alone, or feeling abandoned by God, should not crush us. They should, rather, remind us to turn again to God and to seek God passionately; for certainly God is still near. As in the profound example of Mother Teresa, these times of feeling God's absence should not divert us from our Christian callings or cause us to fall away from our Christian discipleship because in truth we serve the living God and not our feelings—whether they are feelings of God's presence or feelings of God's absence.

Prayer

God, sometimes you seem so near and tangible to me that I can really think of myself as being a coworker with you and my Lord, Jesus Christ. How wonderful it is to feel your nearness! But at other times it feels like you are so far away that I cannot reach you or sense your presence. Grant, Father, that when I feel alone or abandoned, my heart's reaction will not be one of rejection or futility. Remind me that you are not a neglectful Parent to your children, that you care for me, love me, and sustain me even when my feelings seem to say otherwise. For certainly, God, your constancy is far greater than that of my own feelings. Let it be so. In Jesus' name I pray. **Amen.**

Questions for Reflection

1. When have you felt as "cold as an ice block" inside? What did you do about it?

2. Do you think that Mother Teresa's willingness to admit that she sometimes felt no religious feeling inside and yet continued in her work and in her encouragement of others indicated a kind of hypocrisy on her part? Why or why not?

3. Do you see yourself as someone who works with Christ? What difference might this make in the way you approach your life, occupation, family?

4. What value do you place on your feelings when it comes to experiencing God? What other spiritual resources could we turn to for help when feelings fail us?

5. What do you think of the idea that Jesus suffers in the suffering of the poor, hungry, and outcasts? What do you think of Mother Teresa's idea that it is possible to share in these sufferings as well?

For Further Reading

A Gift for God, by Mother Teresa of Calcutta (Harper & Row, Publishers , 1975).

Mother Teresa: Come Be My Light: The Private Writings of the "Saint of Calcutta," edited by Brian Kolodiejchuk, M.C. (Doubleday, 2007).

"Mother Teresa's Crisis of Faith," by David van Biema, in *Time* (Thursday, Aug. 23, 2007), at http://www.time.com/time/printout/0,8816, 1655415.00html.

Notes

[1] From *Mother Teresa: Come Be My Light: The Private Writings of the "Saint Of Calcutta,"* edited by Brian Kolodiejchuk, M.C. (Doubleday, 2007); page 291.
[2] From *Mother Teresa: Come Be My Light*; pages 291–292.
[3] From *Mother Teresa: Come Be My Light*; page 292.
[4] From *Mother Teresa: Come Be My Light*; page 14.
[5] From *Mother Teresa: Come Be My Light*; page 15.
[6] From *Mother Teresa: Come Be My Light*; page 16.
[7] From *A Gift for God*, by Mother Teresa of Calcutta (Harper & Row, Publishers, 1975); pages 20–21.
[8] From *Mother Teresa: Come Be My Light*; pages 39–40.
[9] From *Mother Teresa: Come Be My Light*; page 225.
[10] From *Mother Teresa: Come Be My Light*; pages 1–2.
[11] From *Mother Teresa: Come Be My Light*; page 150.
[12] From *Mother Teresa: Come Be My Light*; page 163.
[13] From *A Gift for God*; page 21.
[14] From *A Gift for God*; page 22.
[15] From *A Gift for God*; page 36.
[16] From *Mother Teresa: Come Be My Light*; page 214.
[17] From *Mother Teresa: Come Be My Light*; page 215.
[18] From *Mother Teresa: Come Be My Light*; page 300.

Made in United States
North Haven, CT
26 September 2023

42026152R00078